# Pray Up
# Your Life

To Elaine
May your faith + power
draw grand blessings
to you in abundance —
now + always,

Charles E. Manuel

# Pray Up Your Life

## 50 Powerful Prayer Practices to Help You Create the Life that You Desire!

Charline E. Manuel

Crystal Heart Press, Inc.

ISBN: 0-9779937-2-8

First Crystal Heart Press, Inc. Hardcover printing April, 2006
Second Printing, Paperback Edition May, 2006

For information regarding special discounts for bulk purchases, contact
Crystal Heart Press, Inc. at crystalheartpress@msn.com

Printed in the United States

*For my mother Elnora Troupe who among many wonderful things, modeled for me the importance of prayer.*

# A Gratitude Moment

I have dreamed of writing a "public" Gratitude Page since I was a little girl. I dreamed that one day I would write a book that would be published and I would celebrate the accomplishment by writing my "acknowledgement" page as my very own gratitude list. I have kept a gratitude journal for many years, so, the writing of this page was the easiest page to write in the entire book.

Abraham Lincoln once said "all that I am I owe to my mother." I could say that too. However, there have been so many others in addition to my mother who added to the person I continually aspire to become. My mother, Elnora had faith that I've only seen in a few people in my life. She went through times of challenge that most people could never even imagine, and yet she believed in God, had great faith, and always believed that no matter what the experience, a prayer would surely help. She continues to be an inspiration to me long after her transition.

My children, Tiffany and Benjamin are my angels from God. They have given me the gift of discovering love. It is my greatest joy to have them call me Mom. I am grateful to my brothers and sisters who have each in their own individual way contributed to my soul growth and development: Bubble, Frances, Elmer, Alberta, Elijah, Catherine and Madison.

My heart is filled with joy for my son in law Abdoulaye who brings a smile to my daughter's face and helped bring forth the gift of my grandson, Madu. I am grateful for the life lessons inspired by the memory of my late husband Carlos.

For all my spiritual teachers who simply encouraged me to keep moving forward no matter what, there have been many, but a few I must mention: the late Maurice Williams, the late David Williamson, the late Jack Boland and Ruth Mosley.

I am so thankful to colleagues who motivate me by the awesome example of Truth by which they live; again there are many, but I must mention a few: Diana McDaniel, Nancy Norman, James Trapp, Robert Marshall and Argentina Glasgow.

For my review, editorial and technical team who freely gave of their time and talents: Tiffany Manuel, Diana McDaniel, Nancy Norman, Karen Morris, Karen Kuebler, Mamie Spring and Akilah Malcolm my heart felt thank you's cannot begin to express my deep gratitude.

Much gratitude goes to my prayer partners on this project. Their prayers helped to pull this book into form: Pinky Sands, Chyrl Ann Forbes, Rosalind Malcolm, Seereah Beckett, Shauna Edwards and Jean Gulliver.

And last but certainly not least my heart is filled with love and gratitude for the entire congregation of Unity Center of Miami. It is the radiating center of love that we are together that helps to make my life so great, grand and awesome.

# Contents

Introduction..................................................................................3

How to Use This Book.................................................................9

### Part 1 *Prayer Practices that Cover the Basics*

Chapter 1.   First Things First..............................................17

Chapter 2.   Pray and Get Ready.........................................23

Chapter 3.   Stay Positive....................................................29

Chapter 4.   Be Persistent – Pray Until Something Happens.......35

Chapter 5.   Practice Seeing................................................41

Chapter 6.   Pray for Your Loved Ones..............................47

Chapter 7.   Prayer Partners................................................53

### Part 2 *Prayer Practices for Special Blessings*

Chapter 8.   Bless Your House............................................61

Chapter 9.   Bless Your Business........................................67

Chapter 10.  Bless Your Pet................................................77

Chapter 11.  Travel Safely..................................................83

Chapter 12.  Claim your Overflowing Blessings.................91

Chapter 13.  Pleasant Words, Healthy Body.......................99

Chapter 14.  When a Loved One Dies...............................105

### Part 3 *Prayer Practices that Add Energy & Power*

Chapter 15.  The Sweet Smell of Answered Prayer...........113

Chapter 16.  Praying with Sacred Symbols.......................119

Chapter 17.  Light a Candle..............................................125

Chapter 18.  Add Soul Stirring Music..............................131

Chapter 19.  The Use of Incense.......................................135

Chapter 20.  Using Precious Stones..................................141

Chapter 21.  Keep a Journal..............................................147

Chapter 22.  Keep a Prayer Vigil......................................153

### Part 4 *Prayer Practices that Help Clear Out Obstacles*

Chapter 23.  Healing Waters.............................................165

Chapter 24.  Dear God Letters..........................................173

Chapter 25.  A Few Words on Forgiveness.......................179

Chapter 26.  Money, Money, Money.................................185

Chapter 27.	A Time to Wait............................................193
Chapter 28.	The Value of A Spiritual Community...............199
Chapter 29.	Praying the Psalms....................................205

*Part 5 Prayer Practices for a Deeper Spiritual Experience*
Chapter 30.	Fast and Pray...........................................215
Chapter 31.	Know your Spiritual Gifts..........................223
Chapter 32.	Chanting.................................................231
Chapter 33.	Breathe..................................................237
Chapter 34.	Pray for a Vision.....................................241
Chapter 35.	A Time to Keep Silence.............................249
Chapter 36.	Make a Covenant with God........................255

*Part 6 Prayer Practices Simply for the Joy of Living*
Chapter 37.	Make a Joyful Noise.................................263
Chapter 38.	Prosperity...............................................269
Chapter 39.	Dance the Prayer You're Praying.................277
Chapter 40.	Go Apart and Rest...................................283
Chapter 41.	Raise Your Gratitude Quotient....................289
Chapter 42.	Love and Romance...................................295
Chapter 43.	The Power of Blessing..............................307

*Part 7 Prayer Practices that Move You Forward for*
*New Opportunities*
Chapter 44.	The Ultimate Prayer of Service....................317
Chapter 45.	Pray for World Peace................................323
Chapter 46.	Letting Go and Moving on..........................331
Chapter 47.	Thank God for Friends..............................343
Chapter 48.	Pray and Move Your Feet...........................349
Chapter 49.	Pray Up the Life You Desire.......................355
Chapter 50.	Let Your Light Shine.................................361

Closing Prayer.............................................................367
Publisher's Page .........................................................369

# Introduction

This book is titled as a true story. That is to say, the 50 powerful prayer practices in this book have blessed my life in countless ways. So when I say that what you have here are "50 Powerful Prayer Practices" I mean just that. I offer them to you, because I know that for the person who is sincere about wanting to grow spiritually, and is willing to put prayer into practice in his/her life, the growth, expansion of consciousness, answers, and revelations desired will surely come. I pray that every area of your life is blessed with your prayerful intention to make it so. May you pray up your life with thoughts, words and actions that reveal God's grace within you and all around you. I pray that you invest great time and energy in creating the life that you desire through God-centered prayer and that you're automatic response to anyone who inquires about your life and affairs is a resounding - Blessed!

There are as many ways to pray as there are people on the planet. Prayer is a personal experience. Quite frankly, I don't think we really need another book on "how to pray" at all. There is sufficient material already in print to teach the basic mechanics of prayer. Yes, some are more detailed than others and each has its own particular approach largely depending on the religious or spiritual views of the author.

Yet, I've discovered there are times along life's pathway that we feel the need to vary our prayer methods to address specific desires we may have. Let's face it, there are times in our lives when "stuff" is happening and we seek something more to help us prayerfully move through that experience. So this book is written not to teach "how to pray," but to complement your prayer life in general.

When you use the prayer practices in this book:

- You'll add a variety of practical, effective methods by which to confirm God's presence within you.
- You'll be reminded that there is no one right way to become aware of the power of God within you.

3

- You'll discover techniques to assist you in developing a prayer consciousness that will result in a life of prayer.
- You'll know what it is to "pray without ceasing".
- You'll consciously create the life you desire to live.

There is another main benefit and blessing to putting these and other prayer practices to work in your life. The more time we spend consciously in prayer, we "Pray Up" the life that we desire for ourselves. I use an investment analogy when I think of "Praying Up" our lives. We invest money in a bank account so that we always have money available to meet our needs. When we "Pray Up" our lives, we invest positive, affirmative prayers into an account, which is our consciousness, and we always have a strong, abundant spiritual bank account capable of handling the desires of our lives.

When we live a life that is "Prayed Up," we joyfully move through our day-to-day experiences with confidence. We know that at all times we are able to draw upon a consciousness that is grounded in the spiritual dominion of unwaivering faith, steadfast love, and the blessed assurance of the power, strength, wisdom and substance to meet our every desire. To abide in this state of consciousness you must *Pray Up Your Life*.

I am among those who believe that every thought, word and act is a form of prayer. I call this our "natural prayer state". We can't help it. We're constantly communicating with God within us all the time. And while we can't change the fact that we're praying all the time, we can change *what* and *how* we are praying.

In Pray Up Your Life, I am referring to prayer as "conscious, intentional communion with God." The more we pray in this fashion, the more we consciously shape our natural prayer state. So this book reveals methods on how you may affect your natural prayer state - every thought, word and act, by increasing your time, energy and effort spent in "conscious, intentional communion with God."

Each chapter of the book has as it's theme a Bible scripture. You'll discover from reading the scriptures alone that there are a variety of methods for prayer for many different purposes. The scripture

4

references provide the foundation from which many of the spiritual practices we use today have their origin. Certainly we have evolved in spiritual consciousness from ancient times, but the innate yearning to know and experience God has not changed one bit. No matter what technique or method we use, we want the same thing today that our ancestors wanted and our avenue for achieving it remains the same, prayer.

Also I wrote this book to address many questions I have received regarding prayer in my role as a minister. For example I've been asked to perform house blessings, car and business blessings. I've been asked if it is OK to pray for money, when the Bible says, "the love of money is the root of all evil?" I've been asked what kinds of prayers one can pray to attract a mate. I've been asked how we can best pray for our loved ones. I've been asked is it OK to use outer symbols, and if so how and if not, why not. I've been asked for suggestions to make prayers more powerful. You get the point.

Sometimes we have particular prayer requests and we want some sound guidance or suggestions on what to do and how to do it. This book reveals what I call prayer practices - practical methods we may incorporate into our spiritual work to support specific areas of interest and concern in our lives.

Over the last twenty years, I have varied my own prayer methods and what occurred as a result is that over time I developed a deeper spiritual foundation and relationship with the God of my being. I am not suggesting that it is the method that necessarily improves our relationship with God, but our methods may support us in developing the habit of conscious, consistent, communion with God. When our relationship with God is strengthened, our faith and trust in God as absolute good deepens. This deeper relationship enhances the outcomes of our prayers.

The various methods in this book helped me to discover that God is my source of all good. I discovered that regardless of the methods I use, I must at least initiate the spiritual laws of life and put them into living practice as conscious communion with God in me.

Each person has his or her own understanding of what prayer is, and how to do it. Most of us learned about prayer during childhood. Many of us continue with those same beliefs and they shape our current prayer habits. Unless we delve deeper into ourselves or make some kind of study of prayer, we generally keep the same habits that we've always had.

For example when I was a child my mother had us kneel before the bed at night to pray. Mostly we said "Now I lay me down to sleep, I pray the Lord my soul to keep, if I should die before I wake, I pray the Lord my soul to take." We could then add "God bless" and name all the members of our family and any friends we wanted to specifically name, and that was it. Well as soon as I was an adult I dropped that cute little prayer, I didn't much like the part "if I should die before I wake." I just didn't want to go to sleep at night thinking about dying. However, I continued the practice of kneeling before my bed to pray for many years into my adulthood and quite frankly sometimes I do indeed kneel when I pray, but not with the belief that this is the only method of saying my nightly prayer. I have discovered that kneeling is not the only way to humble myself in communion with God. Since then, I have given myself permission to invoke other methods of praying and humbling my personal ego to surrender in sweet communion with God.

This book is written primarily out of my own varied experiences in prayer. Every practice in this book I've tried and each one revealed answers and results. But I must caution you, the answers and results were not always as I had hoped or what I had anticipated or planned. However, I developed a wider trust and appreciation for what prayer truly is to me, and that is my constant effort to know and experience God. Let the outcome of your prayers be the unfolding of God's highest good for your life. Always be open to, and willing to be guided by God's plan of absolute good for you and your loved ones.

This book is about giving yourself permission to pray in whatever way feels right for you and that is in alignment with your beliefs and understanding of Truth. Feel free to put your own variation to the prayer practices so that they feel customized for you. Be willing to let the results grow you. Let the answers grow you. Let the works revealed to you, grow you. Isn't that why we pray? So that we may grow into the full realization of all that God created us to be?

With each prayer practice in this book, may you experience the presence of God as your holy self. May you feel the grace and beauty of being fully alive in the sacred chasm of unlimited possibilities. May every prayer find gratitude on your lips, love in your heart and celebration in your soul.

# How Use this Book

This book may certainly be read from beginning to end in sequence. However because of the subject matter you may be guided to read a chapter that addresses some current interest. Many of the prayer practices in the book are related to each other and do in fact complement each other. If you do decide to read it out of sequence, you may want to consider first glancing through some of the other chapters and in particular the chapters in Section 3 "Prayer Practices that Add Energy & Power."

Each chapter in the book opens with a key sentence from the chapter that is the prelude to the lesson. The lesson opens with a scripture that I call the "prayer anchor'" for that particular lesson. It reveals the theme and the background for the particular prayer method listed. All scriptures are taken from the New Revised Standard Version of the Holy Bible except where indicated. Finally each chapter ends with what I call "Prayer Practice," it's how to put the lesson into practical use in your life.

Prayer, as I use it throughout the book, is conscious, intentional communion with God. Sometimes we pray aloud and at other times we may pray silently. When we pray aloud we focus our attention inwardly and speak life-affirming words that heal, bless, prosper and celebrate the life of God working in and through us. We use our words to voice the good that we desire for ourselves and others. We do not spend our words in prayer voicing our challenges, problems and complaints. Words are powerful and so we direct our prayers by carefully choosing the words we speak whether in conscious communion with God or in conversation with others.

When we pray silently, our attention is directed within and we concentrate on words that allow us to fix our thoughts on Truth. We concentrate on divine love, life, wisdom, peace, wholeness, order and faith in God as all good. The more we time we spend in prayer the greater our ability to experience God as the loving presence within us. *Pray Up Your Life* supplies 50 powerful ways to help you consciously pray all the time and for every purpose.

In many of the prayer practices you will be given a certain number of times or days to work with a particular method. I believe as did the ancients regarding numbers. As we read through the Bible and other sacred texts, it is clear that in ancient times numbers had implication beyond their numerical value. For example the number 7 and its derivatives are used more than any other number in the Bible. It is no surprise then, that 7 was believed to be the most sacred of all numbers.

There are other numbers in the scriptures that were used to denote particular significance of inner work. For example a time of 40 days is used to describe deep spiritual times for Moses, Elijah, and Jesus. Surely the writers of the scriptures wanted to draw attention to the spiritual work and its relationship to certain numbers.

We also see the numbers 3 and 12 used very predominantly. In the science of numbers, Numerology, it is revealed that each number has a meaning, purpose and a message. I use the number 9 several times in the prayer practices as it is the number 3 multiplied by its own energy and it is the highest number of the core numbers. Nine is therefore known as the number of completion and higher works. I use it often in this book.

I first became interested in the significance of numbers as used in the scriptures many years ago when I had a revealing dream. I had been going through a very challenging time and went to bed one night in tears crying out to God, what I should do about the situation. In the dream I saw myself celebrating that the situation had been cleared up, I was telling other people in the dream that my problem had been solved after 40 days. Then (still in the dream) I heard "pray for 40 days and the answer will come." When I woke up I wrote the dream in my journal so as not to forget the details. I did as the dream instructed. I took my calendar and numbered it 40 days out. I prayed daily on my request for guidance, and on the fortieth day the answer was so clear that I was at first amazed and then curious. Why 40? It was then that my personal study of the science of numbers began. Not to mention my interest in the study of dreams.

If you find this interesting I would suggest doing some further study into the science of numbers or numerology. Also do some reading of the scriptures that specifically list numbers and study the context in which those numbers are used. For now, I invite you to be conscious of numbers that seem to be prevalent in your life. Most people have what they call a lucky number. I would not subscribe to the idea of luck, but would say that certain numbers do have positive meanings for us in our lives. Unless you are guided otherwise, use the numbers I suggest or numbers that you feel a leaning toward. The idea is for you to have a guide. I also suggest you customize these prayer practices as you are guided.

In the book you will find discussion on outer symbols to enhance your prayer experience. Keep a balance between the outer symbols and your inner work. I cannot stress enough that our work is always inner; the outer symbols can help to enhance the experience, but we must remember that God is our source, and our Source is within.

God answers prayer! You have in your hands tools to help you demonstrate the good that you desire. However, it is important to know that God answers our prayers according to our dominant thoughts, feelings, beliefs and words that we speak. As you work with the various prayer methods in *Pray Up Your Life,* you will condition your mind for the good that you desire; a mind conditioned for good is a magnet for great, grand and awesome experiences to manifest.

God does indeed answer prayer. However, God answers our prayers according to our receptive state of mind, the level of faith in our hearts, our willingness to cooperate with divine order and the power of the Holy Spirit that is constantly active on our behalf as grace. The prayer practices in this book are not quick fixes to life's challenges; they are steady, time-tested, Bible based approaches to support the conscious awareness of God's presence within us. Implement the prayer practices that speak to you, knowing that God, in you, cannot and will not fail.

11

# Part One

# Prayer Practices That Cover the Basics

*God is the beginning, and the beginning is where we must start.*

# 1
## First Things First

_Prayer Anchor:_ _"In the beginning God created the heaven and the earth" (Genesis 1:1)._

When we set a conscious intention to pray, the best decision we can make is to start at the beginning. In the book of Genesis where the allegorical account of creation is told, a great wisdom is revealed that we can use for our benefit. It unveils the importance of having a conscious place to start. One way to look at this is that the Genesis narrative says God started at the beginning. Another way to see it is that God is the beginning. In either case, God is the beginning, and the beginning is where we must start.

When we affirm _In the beginning God_ in our time of prayer, we are setting an intention to co-create with God the desires of our heart. We are positioning ourselves at the point where the creative process begins - with God. We are in effect saying something like, "God is the beginning, God started at the beginning, and that's where I will start too, with God, at the beginning."

This principle of "first things first" is modeled for us in nature. The farmer must prepare the soil first before planting his seeds into the ground. To by-pass this important step would surely affect the quality and quantity of his crops. His harvest would not bring forth the crop that he desired because he did not honor the rule of "first things first." In spiritual matters we follow this principle by acknowledging God first. "But seek first the kingdom of God and His righteousness, and all these things shall be added to you" (Matthew 6:33 NKJV).

When we acknowledge God as the foundation upon which we pray, we are open and receptive to allow God to direct us to the right and perfect answers. This affirms that we want God to be involved in the outcome. In this way, we let ourselves be humble. Without a little humility we might make the error that so many folks make and that is

17

to think that we, apart from God, can achieve the desires of our hearts. We would do well to remember, "It is not I but the Christ within who does the work" (John 14:10). "In the beginning God" admits God into our prayers and acknowledges that we know that we need and want divine guidance and assistance.

If we go back and read the creation story we will see that great patience was taken one day at a time, step by step, to create heaven and earth, living creatures and humankind. And God did not stop until the job was done. "He who began a good work in you will bring it to completion…" (Phil. 1:6). God does not begin something in us only to later abandon it. But God will see it through to completion in us, according to our willingness to follow the steps and stay open to the process.

"God saw everything that he had made, an indeed, it was very good" (Gen. 1:31). So the story goes that after the work was done, God found it favorable and then rested. This is the process we want to follow, we begin with God, follow the steps with great care and patience, know that the creative process is sound and creates according to a divine plan, know that it will be completed in divine order, and then rest in the realization that it is very good. God started at the beginning and took the process through completion and was very pleased with the results.

Isn't that what you want? To start at the beginning, stay the course through completion, and then end up with the outcome that is for your highest good and that of all concerned? Our first prayer practice invites you to engage the creative process beginning with God.

## *Prayer Practice*

In your time of daily prayer, begin by acknowledging God's presence. Establish from the start, that you are consciously aware that God is the foundation of your life and the Source of all that you are, all that you desire to be, have and experience. God first!

As you become consciously aware of God's presence in prayer, turn your attention inwardly. When you experience God as within you,

18

you add great power to your prayer and your ability to follow through on the outcomes you receive. "...for, behold, the kingdom of God is within you" (Luke 17:21 KJV).

Here are a few suggestions on statements you may use at the beginning of your prayer experience to acknowledge God. Select one or all. The idea is to pray from a consciousness that is grounded in the awareness of God. Say these aloud, concentrate on them and meditate on them until you feel centered in God. After you are centered in God's presence within, you are ready to express your prayer desires.

- *"In the beginning, God."* Fix the idea in mind that you are one with God starting out on a prayerful journey within.
- *"I now acknowledge the kingdom of God within me."* As you pray this statement, turn your attention within - focus on your heart, your breathing or toward your abdomen.
- *"God Is, I am."* Repeat this statement until you feel a sense of peace and relaxation knowing that you are one with God.
- *"I AM THAT I AM."* In the Book of Exodus one of the names for God is revealed to Moses. "And Moses said unto God, Behold, when I come unto the children of Israel and shall say unto them The God of our fathers hath sent me unto you; and they shall say to me, What is his name? what shall I say unto them? And God said unto Moses, I AM THAT I AM: and he said, Thus shalt thou say unto the children of Israel, I AM hath sent me unto you" (Exodus 3:13-14 KJV).
- *"I am now consciously aware of God's presence within me."* Whenever you think or speak the words "I am", remember the scripture from Exodus 3:14. "I am" is your personal name for God – only you can say "I am" for you.

As you focus your attention on God within, you are joining the God of your being in a sacred meeting where the creative process is set in motion – the beginning. Be patient and trust that the creative process works and will bring forth results to your prayer in powerful and awesome ways.

*Our beliefs show up in our actions.*

# 2
## Pray and Get Ready

<u>Prayer Anchor:</u> *"So I tell you, whatever you ask for in prayer, believe that you have received it, and it will be yours" (Mark 11:24).*

Ask anyone who prays with a specific request in mind if they believe their prayer will be answered. Most would say 'Yes! I believe'. However, our true beliefs reveal themselves in and through our actions. We can gauge the level of our belief in our answered prayer by listening to our own thoughts, hearing our own words, and observing our actions.

So often I have witnessed others praying for a particular need, say amen and then go right back to talking about how it won't happen, and or doing nothing to prepare for the answer if it were to manifest. To pray and believe means that we consciously open ourselves up in communion with God on a matter and then we trust that our highest good will manifest. We don't second-guess the situation, we move forward as though it is already done. Amen!

I once was acquainted with a young woman who prayed for male companionship. She was praying, made a treasure map (a prayer desire displayed in pictures), and had asked others to pray with her. After several months of all this effort, a young man new to the church that we both attended asked her to attend a work-related social function with him. Well I was shocked when she told me she declined the invitation. When I asked her why, she had a list of excuses like: she had nothing to wear, she didn't feel comfortable with their first date being a large gathering, and she did not have time to get her hair done before the event, and on and on and on. If she had believed her prayer would indeed manifest as she was praying all those months, she would have been preparing in every conceivable way to say yes to an opportunity when it did indeed arise.

23

The words we put out in prayer must be an inner embrace of that which we are praying about. In other words, our beliefs show up in our actions! If we truly believe that what we pray for can be ours, and is ours, we will automatically pray and move our feet toward their manifestation. If we believe, really believe, we would not let minor excuses become obstacles to opportunities that arise as a result of our prayers.

The epilogue to the story is that the young man when declined by the young woman, asked another woman in the church who said yes. They begin dating and two years later were married.

Now it certainly is true that all is in divine order with regard to who ended up with whom, but the point is, if we pray it, we should be ready or at least get ready for what we are praying for. Our job is to pray and get ready. We pray and immediately prepare for the opportunities that will present themselves as possible answers to our prayer.

When we pray we create and send forth an energy field that begins to work on our behalf. This young man may not have been "the one" but his appearance did demonstrate that she was sending out positive energy for what she was praying about. However when we are not prepared for a response to our prayer, we send forth a mixed vibrational signal regarding what we desire. If the young man was not of a quality of character that she desired in a companion, it was proper that she redirect his advances. However to reject his advances with "NO, I have nothing to wear," speaks to being unprepared for that which she had been praying for. We must pray and get ready!

## *Prayer Practice*

Periodically check your level of belief. Take the prayer anchor for this chapter into your time of prayer and meditate on the words. Concentrate on its meaning to you. Determine if your outer actions are in alignment with what you are praying. Observe your thoughts, words, and actions to see if they do indeed reflect what you are praying. If not, this is an area you need to work on. If they do, when you pray begin immediately preparing for the demonstrations that you are sure to draw as a result of your prayers and beliefs being in alignment.

Pray with your whole heart for that which you desire to manifest in your life. Use the techniques in this book and others that you know. Whether you speak your prayers aloud, affirm them in the silence of your being, write them in your prayer journal, or pray them with your prayer group, when you act as though you believe the prayer is a living reality, you cooperate with the spirit of God within you to bring the prayer into manifestation.

Whenever our prayers are delayed, the first place to examine ourselves is in the area of belief. Your part in manifesting your desire is to pray and believe. Pray your prayers and move your feet – like you really believe it will be!

*When we make positive thinking a habit, the prayers we pray can only draw to us positive results.*

# 3
## Stay Positive

*Prayer Anchor:* *"Finally, beloved, whatever is true, whatever is honorable, whatever is just, whatever is pure, whatever is pleasing, whatever is commendable, if there is any excellence and if there is anything worthy of praise, think about these things" (Philippians 4:8).*

Our mind power to decide what we will think, what we will say, and what we will do is truly one of God's greatest gifts. I can remember times in my life when I was firm on a decision that I had made and with unwavering persistent faith, miraculous things happened. I had set in mind an intention, a decision made, and my outer circumstances cooperated with my mental choice.

One such time was when I decided to go back to school to get my Master's degree. I had just moved to Kansas City the previous year with my son who was just five years old at the time. I had no family there and knew only a few people I worked with and a few friends in my church family. The challenge was who would baby-sit while I took classes at night. During the day Benjamin was in school, but evenings posed what seemed to be a difficulty at the time. I remember the day I registered for classes thinking, "I don't know how I'm going to do this without something in place for my son's care," but I registered anyway.

Up until the night of my first class I had no one to look after Benjamin. I fed him dinner praying the whole time something like "Dear God I know I'm going to class tonight and I know that Benjamin will be safely cared for, I just don't know how yet, but I know there is an answer." Even Benjamin was concerned. He must have asked 10 times or more, "Where am I going when you go to school? Am I going with you? Who's going to keep me?"

Just after we had dinner there was a knock at the door and it was a little boy and his mom who lived a few buildings away from our apartment building. Benjamin had played with the boy outside, and I only knew his mother well enough to say hello in passing and to wave to when the boys were at play. The boy and his mother came to invite Benjamin to their home that evening. It was the boy's birthday and the mom was inviting only a few of the neighborhood boys over for ice cream and cake and to play a few games. I told her I had to attend a class that night and would not be back until about 9:00 p.m. She said that was fine. Well that was the start of what became a friendship with this woman who kept Benjamin when I had night classes. On Saturdays when she needed to run errands I kept her son, with Benjamin and me. I could not have planned a better arrangement myself.

But that experience taught me the power of a made-up mind. I had decided I was going back to school and the details were worked out beyond what I could have ever imagined.

One of the tools for helping us to form our desires in mind is focus. Focus can propel us toward our desires in miraculous ways. When we focus on what we want rather than what we do not want, we set in motion the power to bring into manifestation the desires of our hearts. With conscious, faithful, and persistent focus of our thoughts, we become magnets for unseen possibilities to find us. The process of affirmations, positive statements of truth, and denials, (statements that refute negative thoughts from our minds) help us to form the quality of thoughts that draw to us the good that we desire.

So often it appears that our prayers are not answered and the truth is that we were not clear, definite, or specific about what we were praying for in the first place. Affirmations and denials help us to get into the mental space of knowing what we desire. Once the desire is clear in mind, we anchor the desire in mind with the steady flow of positive thoughts. When we make positive thinking a habit, the prayers we pray can only draw to us positive results.

## _Prayer Practice_

The prayer anchor for this chapter can be extremely helpful in training ourselves to think on the positive side of things. For 9 days, write the scripture as though you are writing a letter to yourself. Write it out this way 3 times each of the 9 days as early in the morning as you can:

_Finally, beloved_____(your name), today, _____(day and date) set your mind on whatever is true, whatever is honorable, whatever is just, whatever is pure, whatever is pleasing, whatever is commendable, if there is any excellence and if there is anything worthy of praise, think about these things."_

Afterwards, prayerfully read the scripture in your own handwriting first aloud, the second time softly and the third time, think it to yourself. Then spend a few minutes in silent concentration on this scripture.

This is a mind-conditioning prayer. It will help you form positive thought as a habit and way of approaching your life situations. If you do have a particular prayer request that you are working with and staying positive is a challenge for you, say this scripture as a prayer three times before you give your attention to your specific request.

Spend your days thinking about your affairs in the highest positive way that you can. If you find yourself falling into negative thinking, recite the scripture to yourself a few times to get back on track. You'll be amazed at the difference this can make if you are indeed sincere about wanting to change the quality of your thinking toward a more positive, conscious way of being.

31

*As we pray persistently,
with each time that
we affirm our desire,
we become
increasingly assured
of a blessed outcome.*

# 4
## Be Persistent - Pray Until Something Happens

*Prayer Anchor:* *"And he said to them, "Suppose one of you has a friend, and you go to him at midnight and say to him, 'Friend, lend me three loaves of bread; for a friend of mine has arrived, and I have nothing to set before him.' And he answers from within, 'Do not bother me; the door has already been locked, and my children are with me in bed; I cannot get up and give you anything;' I tell you, even though he will not get up and give him anything because he is his friend at least because of his persistence he will get up and give him whatever he needs" (Luke 11:5-8).*

Jesus tells this parable as a lesson in persistence. If our desires are worth anything to us, then certainly they are worthy of our persistent attention and consistent efforts. Our intention becomes to pray until something happens toward the manifestation of our prayer.

Repetition or persistently affirming a particular prayer until it is satisfied is a technique that has been effective throughout the ages. Joshua had the children of Israel walk around the walls of Jericho 7 times before it fell; Elijah had his servant look for rain 7 times before it rained. In the 119th Psalm, the Psalmist says he praises God 7 times each day. Daniel prayed 3 times a day. In ancient times The Lord's Prayer was prayed 15 times resulting in healings and demonstrations of abundant blessings.

First of all, you can never pray too much or too often. In fact we are praying all the time in the normal course of our day, we just don't call it prayer. Our thoughts are prayers, and as we hold thoughts in our minds, they get busy producing after their own kind.

However, when you have a prayer for which you desire to see something specifically manifest, persistent prayer can be the approach to take. In this prayer method you are praying the same prayer until you see some results or until you feel a sense of total peace regarding your desire.

In the prayer anchor for this chapter, Jesus tells the story of a friend who knocks on the door at midnight. The family is already in bed and the man of the house does not want to disturb the household by answering the door. But the friend knocks at the door with great persistence. He desires help and will not let the family rest peacefully until he gets what he desires.

When we make a decision to pray until we get some results we have the attitude of the friend who persisted. Just as he knocked once and then twice and however many times it took, to receive his desire, we too can use that same kind of perseverance to attain what we desire. We can apply that same kind of strength of mind toward our desires until we feel the movement of spirit on behalf of our prayer.

The key to repetition and persistence in our prayer desire is not to lose heart. We must be so grounded in our faith that we keep praying until we see, feel, and know that some change has and is occurring. Do not be easily discouraged. Do not give up if nothing appears to happen as soon as you think that it should. "Then Jesus told them a parable about their need to pray always and not to lose heart" (Luke 18:1).

Remember that Spirit is at work though you may not see the outer result of that work yet. Your part is to not give up, not to quit but to do your work as Spirit is working also. "But Jesus answered them, My Father is still working and I also am working" (John 5:17). **As we pray persistently, with each time that we affirm our desire, we become increasingly assured of a blessed outcome.**

In our church we conduct a 'Pray Until Something Happens' prayer vigil each year, it usually is set for anywhere from 99 to 120 days. Each person sets an intention toward specific prayer desires and that some movement toward achievement will occur during the time set for the vigil. The idea is to practice persistent, faithful repetition of

36

our prayer desire, expecting something great, grand, and awesome to occur.

Each person is given a mustard seed as a reminder of the importance of faith throughout the process. They receive a card numbered up to the scheduled number of days set for the vigil. Each person will check off a day at a time for the days remaining. Many people have put notes on the bathroom mirror, or on the refrigerator, pictures in their wallet, you name it, all to stay focused and committed to something happening toward their desire. It is always a joy to hear the many expressions of gratitude for demonstrations made as a result of persistent prayer.

When we trust the spirit of God within, giving our time, attention, faith, expectation and persistent effort, something must and will unfold. To set an intention and commitment to pray until something happens is a powerful process that can yield blessings beyond our imagination.

## _Prayer Practice_

This prayer practice is about setting an intention to be persistent in your prayer work. This can take the form of setting a specific time of day for your daily prayer. You could establish the number of times a day you will pray as well as decide on a specific prayer or format for your prayer. This all depends on your commitment and your level of desire.

If reading the prayer anchor daily helps to keep you focused toward persistent action, then by all means do so. Persistent, positive, faith-filled prayer is your work until you reach your desire.

Get clear on your prayer desire. Consider writing out your desire. This will help to clarify and to assure that you are praying the same prayer each time. Decide how many times you will pray the prayer each day and the number of days, or until something happens within you.

The idea of praying until something happens is reaching that point within you when you feel complete with the prayer and that it is done. You may sense a readiness within for the outer manifestation of it. You may arrive at a mental state within where you feel it is no longer desirous or necessary to pray the prayer. There can be a range of revelations such as discovering that the prayer is no longer a desire, that your desires have changed over the course of the prayer and/or Spirit may have something better in store.

The important thing is that you stay open to all possibilities but your intention is that "something" will happen as a result of your persistent prayers and you have the faith and assurance that whatever does happen will be for your highest good.

Focus is important and a major help in staying persistent in your prayer efforts. I suggest using what I call a focus tool to help. This may be keeping a 'pray until something happens journal.' With each day that you pray your desire, you write something regarding the manifestation of your desire. For example if your prayer desire was for a new car, you might write in your journal the kinds of things you'll do when you have the car, places you'll go, people you see riding with you in the car, etc. You'll write about aspects of the manifest desire that will be exciting, fun, and uplifting for you. Focus is the key to maintaining perseverance.

Set your intentions before you start this prayer practice. Put your energy into living out those intentions each day until you see a change, results, transformation, miracles, or some level of personal satisfaction that you have set for yourself. Prayer changes us and the more we focus our time, energy, commitment, and faith in prayer, we can be assured that indeed something can and will happen on our behalf and it will be good and very good!

*When we can see
what we desire with our
eyes closed, we activate
the power to see it
with our eyes open.*

# 5
## Practice Seeing

*Prayer Anchor:* *"Lift up your eyes, and look from the place where you are, northward and southward and eastward and westward; for all the land which you see I will give to you...." (Genesis 13:14).*

This wonderful scripture tells us that our Creator has instituted the laws of life so that if we use what God has given us, in this case the ability to imagine, we can actually demonstrate that which we see. We can use this mind power to imagine in mind that which we desire and thereby cooperate with divine law in shaping what we draw to us in experience. If you close your eyes this moment, can you see the life you desire? Can you see the prayer request you desire already fulfilled? Can you see with your eyes closed pictures of the things you desire to have?

When I was a child in elementary school, I was often labeled as being a daydreamer. I sometimes would not finish my assignments because I would be staring out the window dreaming of all kinds of experiences. I think one of my favorite things to do as a child was to stare out the window. I could do it for hours. By the time I reached high school however, I had set aside my tendency to just sit and stare out the window and daydream. Little did I know as a child that I was developing my faculty of imagination and the powerful spiritual tool of visualization. The God-given ability we have to see things that are not physically visible to the human eye is the mighty power we have to imagine.

When you dream at night while you are asleep, you see pictures with your eyes closed. You may have even seen something in a dream before it actually happened. This confirms for us that the mind can and does have the ability to show pictures on the screen of our minds even before they can be seen in the outer realm.

41

Little did I know as I was daydreaming, I was developing my ability to visualize and thereby give power to the manifestation of what I desired. When we think with specific pictures in mind toward some experience we'd like to have, we are using the powerful mental tool of day dreaming, visualizing or picturing to utilize our faculty of imagination. It strengthens our conscious ability to hold a picture in mind. Once we impress on the conscious and subconscious levels of mind, what we hold in mind is drawn to us.

Some folks have a little more difficulty with using the imagination to see pictures in their minds. In this case, using outer pictures can be helpful to train the mind to see pictures inwardly. The idea is simply to look at pictures with your physical eye until you can close your eye and see the same picture and then begin to create pictures in your mind about whatever else you desire to bring into manifestation. What we see with feeling and strong desire we can expect to draw to us.

Many of us are prone to daydreaming. Once we begin to understand this great power that we have, we will not spend endless hours imagining what we do not wish to demonstrate in our lives. But rather begin to practice seeing what we truly desire.

Some have a stronger ability to close their eyes and see things that have not yet manifested in the physical realm. Others must put more practice into being able to see ideas in mind. Creative folks like artists, designers, architects and others have a more developed gift for seeing a picture in mind and then putting it into a visible form for others to see. This is a technique that we can use to bring the good that we desire into manifestation: visualization.

Try this exercise: Find a picture that represents something you would like to have or experience. Look at the picture for a few minutes with admiration and desire. Now, imagine a movie screen on the inside of your forehead. Practice seeing the outer picture on your inner mental screen. Don't try to force the experience. Again look at the picture for a few minutes then close your eyes again and practice seeing the picture on your mental screen. Do this several times until you can see the picture with your eyes closed. The more you do this kind of exercise the better you will be at doing it and thereby give power to the prayers you picture in mind.

Visualization is one of the first spiritual tools I learned to use after discovering Unity School of Christianity. Many years ago when I first started seriously reading Unity's publication, the Daily Word, I saw an advertisement: "Spiritual Retreats." Immediately I knew I wanted to go to Unity Village in Missouri for the experience. At the time there appeared to be obstacles to my taking a week-long trip away from my young daughter and my job. At the time, finances were not in place for such a trip. I got a picture of Unity Village and in my prayer time each day I saw myself approaching the facility. It was just a few months later that the funds I needed to go, the time off from my job, and the babysitter I needed for my young daughter all fell into place smoothly. It fell together so easily; I knew I was meant to go. It was just the beginning of a long list of how grateful I am to have found Unity.

The prayer anchor for the chapter reads: "Lift up your eyes." When we look away from the physical as it is, we look up in consciousness and see that which has not yet taken physical form for us. **When we can see what we desire with our eyes closed, we activate the power to see it with our eyes open.** That which we see inwardly makes an impression on the mind and what is held in mind draws its outer equivalent into physical reality.

## _Prayer Practice_

The idea here is to see yourself fully enjoying the good that you are praying for. See it in your mind's eye as you would like to experience it. Collect pictures of that which you desire to demonstrate as a result of your specific prayer. Visualize yourself in the picture. Select pictures that are in color and attractive to the eye, they will make more of an impression on your mind. When you look at the picture it should arouse your desire for that which you are praying about. It is important that you see yourself in the picture doing, being and having the experience that you desire.

In your visualization you may string a series of pictures together and form your own movie with other characters, music, etc. Be the star of the movie as well as the director. When you feel you have sufficiently experienced your desire within, to the point of feeling that it is real, then you have visualized your prayer. Close your time of prayerful visualization with a statement that is something like: *"I am grateful for this or whatever is for my greatest good and in accordance with God's divine plan for me."*

Daily use your pictures during your prayer time. With your eyes closed, practice seeing yourself experiencing the desire you are praying about. Speak aloud prayer statements that support your desires such as "I am _____(fill in your prayer statement)..." or "I see myself_____(fill in the blank)".

Use the pictures until you have it firmly envisioned in your mind. When you can close your eyes and see yourself with that which you desire you may release the pictures and rely on your faculty of imagination. With a strong command of your faculty of imagination and the practice of seeing your desires, you'll be able to move mountains.

*Most religious and spiritual movements teach and practice some method of praying for others.*

# 6
## Pray For Your Loved Ones

*Prayer Anchor:* *"I thank my God every time I remember you, constantly praying with joy in every one of my prayers for all of you" (Philippians 1:3).*

Since none of us exists in the world alone, it should be a routine practice for us to pray for those who are closest to us – family, friends, and those we consider our loved ones. Some folks are so close to us and play such a valuable part in our lives that our lives are greatly affected by their health, happiness, and well-being. To pray for them is only natural. Moreover, to pray for them on a regular basis is just plain wise and loving.

There is a more personal side of why we pray for others. If we want a steady flow of good circulating in our lives, we should indeed make it a habit of regularly and consistently praying for others. Each time we pray for someone else we are blessed in the process as well. It's a double blessing when we pray for others.

Throughout the scriptures, we see friends, families and members of spiritual communities praying with and for each other. **Most religious and spiritual movements teach and practice some method of praying for others.** This reminds us of the importance of praying for others and particularly those closest to us.

Do you remember in the garden of Gethsemane where Jesus asks the disciples to pray with him? This lets us know that no matter who we are we appreciate prayers from our loved ones and particularly those closest to us.

Let me say a few words about how to pray for loved ones. It is not in spiritual integrity to pray for specific outcomes for your loved ones without their permission to do so. I remember many years ago a young woman asked me to pray with her that her boyfriend's wife would give him a divorce so that they could be married. While she assured me that it was indeed his desire to leave his wife for her, I took notice that she showed up alone to make such a request. I could not pray any such prayer regarding this situation. I did pray a prayer of divine order with her. We joined together in affirming that God's will be manifest for all concerned in the situation. She left not very happy with the prayer but I could not and would not presuppose to know the inner desires of all those involved in this situation and did not choose to do so.

Whenever we pray for others, we must surrender our personal will and trust that a larger plan exists for their lives than what we are privy to. I once had a woman come to me to ask that her son find a nice girl, settle down, and get married. This is what she wanted for him. Again, I prayed a prayer of divine order with her. Some years later I spoke with her only to learn that her son was gay and had been afraid to tell her. When we pray for others, we must trust that God knows beyond our human awareness and personal understanding the intricate details that are not ours to know.

While there may be times when we feel compelled to be intricately involved in the lives of our loves one, it may be that our best support for them, is to trust God on their behalf. We can always pray what I believe to be the highest prayer that we can pray for ourselves or anyone else. "Father, thy will be done."

## *Prayer Practice*

Find a prayer that you particularly like in praying for your loved ones and pray it every day. You may decide to pray the Lord's Prayer on their behalf, the $23^{rd}$ Psalm, or any other prayers that you find that suits your spiritual understanding. There are many books of prayer where you can select prayers that are right for you and your loved ones or you may simply compose a prayer of your own.

Prayers of protection, guidance, and peace are part of my personal prayer practice for my loved ones. Every day I pray the same prayer for them. I may change a word here and there from time to time, but overall I want God's light, love, and presence to surround and enfold them wherever they are. Regardless of what is going on in their affairs, my prayer is consistent and a sincere desire for God's will not mine, to be done in their lives.

Consistency is important. Focusing daily attention on the well-being of your loved ones will be more helpful than a sporadic reaction to life's challenges. Make your prayer for your loved ones a daily habit and an important part of your personal prayer practices.

In the 17th Chapter of the Book of John, Jesus models a 3-step process of first praying for himself, second praying for those closest to him, and third praying for all others. Do not underestimate the good you can do by daily taking the time to hold your loved ones in prayer. We may not be able to physically do anything to help those we love through life's challenges, but we can always say a prayer on their behalf and prayer is powerful and transforming.

*Having a prayer partner or partners in no way diminishes or demeans the power we gain in silent communion alone with God.*

# 7
## Prayer Partners

*Prayer Anchor:* "For where two or three are gathered in my name, I am there among them" (Matthew 18:20).

If you've read this far into this book, you may have an interest in having a prayer life that continually expands your consciousness and allows you to live up to your true potential. As illustrated in this book, there are many methods you can use to enhance your prayers. Yet nothing will enhance your prayers more than having a like-minded prayer partner or a group of like-minded people who pray with you and whom you pray for on a regular basis.

In Jesus' teachings we find spiritual principles by which to live our lives, but Jesus also modeled His teachings by His actions. On several occasions, Jesus met with his prayer partners for prayer support. In Matthew 17, Jesus took Peter, James, and John and led them up a high mountain by themselves. The high mountain represents a prayerful state of consciousness, where they went to be alone and pray together. In this particular instance, the scripture goes on to describe the result of that powerful prayer experience. It reads, "his face shone like the sun, and his clothes became dazzling white." Pretty powerful results! Jesus had a vision from God that was revealed to him and it was so powerful that it changed him from within and reflected in his outer appearance in the presence of his prayer partners. We know that prayer does not change God; it changes us. We want to be changed so that we may be more of a channel for the goodness of God to manifest in our lives.

This brings us to the value in having two or three like-minded others who can see us transform into that which is in alignment with our prayers. Our prayer partner can see us with spiritual insight and faith. This gives our prayers greater power than if we were praying without them.

Having a prayer partner or partners in no way diminishes or demeans the power we gain in silent communion alone with God. It is another method we may use to expand our consciousness of prayer. Certainly Jesus had times when he prayed alone as a testimony to the importance of our alone time with God. Yet, there were times when he wanted the prayer support of others.

There may be a time for you when your prayer partners can only give you their presence; they can simply be available and accessible to you, and that may be the added support that you need at the moment. Did you ever say to someone "I'll be there for you"? There can be great support in just showing up, being there for someone else or having them be there for us.

Sometimes folks are reluctant to ask for prayer. Sometimes we'd rather suffer silently than to let someone else know that we need help because we think it is a sign of weakness. Yet if we want to truly demonstrate our inner strength, we must ask for help when we need it and when we want it. In so doing, we find an inner courage that immediately empowers us to find the solutions and answers we desire. Jesus tells us, and models for us that prayer partnering is a tool that we may use. In essence, we can harness greater power by praying with others.

## *Prayer Practice*

Select your prayer partner or partners carefully and prayerfully. You want a person who is like-minded and who you know can and will support you without criticism, judgment, or shaming. This is one of the values in being a member of a spiritual community. You will be drawn to certain people within that community and certain others will be drawn to you. Your chances of finding someone who is suited to you as a partner to pray with are enhanced within your spiritual network.

When you find someone who you feel may be a possible candidate for you as a prayer partner, discuss with them the idea of partnering in prayer. Have a discussion about confidentiality on what is shared so that you each feel comfortable in expressing your true concerns in prayer. Establish that the group's purpose is for prayer support not for advice-giving or any kind of counseling. Let your desires be made known and ask them how they would like to be supported if indeed you were to pursue such a relationship. The two of you might even pray together about the decision to become prayer partners.

Suggest a time length for the relationship such as 2 months. This will allow you both to determine if you want to make a longer commitment to each other as partners.

Once you've found a partner or partners, set a regular time when you are to meet in person or contact each other by phone for your time of prayer. It is best to set a time frame within which the prayer is to take place. If there is no set time limit, talking will go on and on and eventually the prayers become less and the talking becomes more. Consider once a week for about 15 -30 minutes.

Agree on a format that will work for both of you. You may use an inspirational reading, scripture or a structured method that you both agree on. Once the format is set, just do it! Great, grand, and awesome things happen when we gain the added prayer power of another like-minded person or persons, so expect awesome demonstrations to happen, and they will.

# Part Two

# Prayer Practices
# For special blessings

*I remember thinking as a child "when I grow up, I'm not going to make my children do all this hard work." Guess what?*

# 8
## Bless Your House

*Prayer Anchor: "He said to them, 'It is written, 'my house shall be called a house of prayer'" (Matthew 21:13).*

When I was a little girl, we used to sing a song that had the words: "Bless this house Oh Lord we pray, make it safe by night and day..." Even then I had an early belief in the benefits of blessing the house where one lives. The space where we take our meals, enjoy our family and friends, sleep at night to rest our bodies and renew our minds, is a sacred space and deserves the treatment of a sacred and holy place.

There are many good books written on space clearing and spiritual cleansing so I will not try to imitate what has been done well by so many others. If you are not already in the habit of regularly clearing and cleansing the space in your home, I recommend that you seek out some of these books and begin putting into practice this principle of clearing, cleansing, blessing, and praying up your house.

Also when I was a little girl, my mother had us do something called spring-cleaning. We would throw out old stuff we were no longer using or things that no longer worked. My mother would open all the windows and doors in the house on a Saturday in early springtime and all of us kids would be put to work. Using the smelly cleaning products my mother insisted we use, like ammonia, bleach, vinegar, etc., we would wash windows, walls, scrub floors, clean the crystal chandelier in the dining room, wash the bedding and towels and hang them on the clothes line outside to air out. Then there would be the cleaning of the kitchen. All the pots and pans would be taken out of the cabinets and the inside of the cabinets were cleaned out so that we could rearrange the contents in the cabinets. I remember thinking as a child "When I grow up I'm not going to make my children do all this hard work." Guess what? I did and, yes they complained.

But what I do remember enjoying is the fresh clean smell and feel the house had after all the work was done. The house had a light and airy feel to it. It seemed like the way you'd want the house to be all the time. Perhaps you can relate to this.

Even today, I enjoy my home when it is orderly, clutter free, clean, smelling good with fragrances that uplift the spirit and my belongings arranged in a way that is aesthetically pleasing to the eye. I enjoy being in my home and truly feel better no matter how my day at the office has gone. Home feels safe, healthy, and uplifting.

In this chapter, I want to stress the importance of keeping your home free from clutter, keeping it clean, clearing the energy within it and praying it up. I have often been asked to perform a house blessing for people when they first move into a new home. And I have done it on many occasions. However, I believe the best person to bless your house is you. This way, you set your own intentions and make your own vibration, the one your house reflects. Also a house blessing is not a one-time thing. I believe a house blessing should be done regularly a few times a year, after some event of a challenging nature occurs in the home, or when the home is in harm's way - like when a hurricane, tornado or storm is headed your way.

There are certain circumstances when you may want a professionally trained person in space-clearing to do this kind of work for you. Examples are when the energy is extremely heavy or negative after a traumatic situation has occurred in the home, i.e. someone is tragically killed, a home invasion, or the previous inhabitants were living a negative lifestyle and you just bought the house.

Yes, there are people who do this kind of work. I am thinking more of spiritual or Feng Shui practitioners. Get suggestions from those in your spiritual community or some New Age stores may be able to recommend a person who is skilled at this work. However, anyone you know with a strong prayer consciousness will be a good candidate to assist you. My caution is to use good wisdom in selecting the person. Pray to be guided to the right and perfect person.

61

Have a consecrated space in your home where you perform your daily prayers. This may include setting up an altar or several altars in your home to help facilitate your prayer efforts. Once your space is cleared of clutter and negative energy, pray the space up. Make your house a house of prayer by praying in it, for it, and all through it.

The main thing to remember is to keep your house in order and filled with positive energy. Learn some of the various cleansing ceremonies and rituals for clearing space; they may become a part of your regular spiritual practices.

## *Prayer Practice*

I recommend including a scripture as part of your house blessing. I use The Lord's Prayer, the 23rd and 91$^{st}$ Psalm. You may use other blessings along with these, but I like beginning my blessing with scripture to give my house blessing my own favored spiritual foundation.

This is the basic house blessing I suggest you give your home once or twice a year. Be sure to do a blessing when you occupy your home for the first time. You may choose to do a blessing after something has happened to cause you to believe there may be some blocked or negative energy in your home. Once you have done this level of blessing, you will probably just do a maintenance blessing once or twice a year.

- Use incense to clear the energy throughout the entire house. Set a mental intention that you are clearing away any negative or stale energy in your home. Walk the inner perimeter of the house slowly and gently waving the stick of incense. I suggest using frankincense & myrrh, sage, or sandalwood.

- Light a white candle in each room. If possible place the candle in the center of the room. Allow it to burn for several hours after the blessing is complete.

- From the outside of your home, face the main entrance to your home and pray the 23rd Psalm. Proceed to the inside, facing the main entrance headed outside, again pray the 23$^{rd}$ Psalm. Now from the inside, pray the 23$^{rd}$ Psalm facing each entrance door of your house until every entrance and exit has been blessed with this Psalm.

- Next, starting from the inside of your front door, pray the 91$^{st}$ Psalm as you walk from room to room.

- Pray the Lord's Prayer aloud in its entirety in every room of your house.

- Now begin speaking words of protection, health, and well-being in each room regarding the purpose of the space. Bless the kitchen for healthy, nourishing meals to be prepared there with love. Bless the bathrooms for divine elimination (Yes do it; it is important for good health). Bless the family room for good quality family time together in harmony, peace, and fun. For all those who live in the house, use their names when you bless the rooms where they sleep. For example, when I blessed my son's room after we first moved into our new home, I said something like: *'I am grateful that Benjamin is always divinely guided, guarded and protected wherever he is, and that this room is a restful, peaceful happy place for him."* (I should have added something about the cleanliness of it, but his room has always been a safe haven for him so I don't complain). Make up your own prayer for each room. Just speak from your heart the highest intentions you have for those who will occupy the space. *Affirm that God's grace is always present and active in the space, now and always.*

Allow the candles you have placed to burn completely out. Place some fresh flowers in the main living areas of the house for the next 3 days. Enjoy the peaceful blessed energy you have created in your home.

An exception to the once or twice a year house blessing is during times of preparation for severe weather conditions like hurricanes, tornadoes, and other storms. I recommend that you bless your home praying the 91$^{st}$ Psalm as you walk around the entire outside perimeter of your home. Then on the inside, from the center point of the home affirm aloud the Lord's Prayer followed by the 23rd Psalm. Finally, facing each of the four corners of the house, pray the 91$^{st}$ Psalm.

As an ongoing spiritual practice, speak kind and loving words in every room of your house on a regular basis. Fill the air with healthy, peaceful energy, and consecrate your house as a house of prayer.

*When we get the real ownership issue handled regarding whose business we intend to operate, we're on our way to success.*

# 9
# Blessing Your Business

*Prayer Anchor: "And he said unto them, How is it that ye sought me? wist ye not that I must be about my Father's business?" (Luke 2:49 KJV).*

Most of us at one time or another dream up some great invention, a clever product or an idea that we would just love to sell to the whole world. In the dream, our business would succeed where others have failed. We would have the ideal product, the best people to work for us, the perfect plan, and the money, fame, accolades and fortune to prove it.

While dreams do often manifest for us, we've also seen the dreams of the 'mom and pop' operations fold, and we've seen big businesses forced to file for bankruptcy. Every year many businesses go belly up, and are forced to close their doors. And, we probably could not begin to imagine the many thousands of businesses that are just getting by or operating in the red.

I remember many years ago, I went to a seminar on starting your own business. The seminar leader said up front, "Quite frankly I want to talk you out of starting your own business. Most people have a romantic idea of what business ownership is and the reality is that owning a business is tough business." When I left the seminar that day, I had the sense that entrepreneurship could be a great blessing or my worst nightmare.

Yet each year many new businesses spring up with fresh enthusiasm for a chance at successful entrepreneurship. There is something fascinating about starting a new venture that we believe in. There is a special kind of energy that propels the person who is inclined to pursue the manifestation of his/her idea into a living enterprise. I've felt it, maybe you have to. Some of us even have what I call the "entrepreneur gene."

67

I first became aware of the entrepreneur gene by observing my mother. She had it. Her dream was to be a restaurant owner and she became that several times. I worked in her restaurants as a young girl and had the opportunity to observe her passion, drive, and enthusiasm for her dream. She worked long hours and holidays and never was it a chore. My mother loved to cook and she did it with love. She was a good cook, her food was delicious, and her ideas were grand. I can truly say that she enjoyed what she did. Even up until the time she made her transition, she continued to talk about new ideas for the next restaurant she wanted to open.

I don't think that everyone who starts their own business has the entrepreneur gene, and I don't think they have to. I do however, believe that we should all love what we do as our livelihood and that it helps to have passion, drive, and enthusiasm for any venture we expect to thrive in. Even still, we need something more if we want to be fulfilled by the work involved and successful in our own business venture.

In the prayer anchor for this chapter, Jesus is a young boy, but he gives us sound advice that we can use for successfully owning and running a business of any kind. His parents had been searching for Jesus as he was separated from them a few days prior. They found the boy in the temple doing what seemed to be natural to him and would later prove to be what he had passion, drive and enthusiasm for. His parents, obviously concerned for his well-being in the previous days, ask him what he's doing. He says to them, "I must be about my Father's business." This is the success ingredient that when embraced, can assist in the fulfillment and success we desire in whatever business we're guided to embark upon.

Jesus gets to the core with this statement. If we start a business, who is really the head of it? Who is its true owner? When we get the real ownership issue handled regarding whose business we intend to operate, we're on our way to success.

If we do acknowledge the business idea as a divine idea, coming to us and through us as God's idea, we will have an attitude grounded in success. When we agree to take God's idea and be the hands and feet that will bring it into manifestation, we are then setting out in business not alone, but with the most powerful and awesome business owner available to all humankind. God never fails and neither can we if we are as Jesus said, "about our Father's business."

In 1 Chronicles, King David models what being about our Father's business looks like: "Then David blessed the Lord in the presence of all the assembly; David said: "Blessed are you, O Lord, the God of our ancestor Israel, forever and ever. Yours, O lord are the greatness, the power, the glory, the victory, and the majesty; for all that is in the heaven and on the earth is yours; yours is the kingdom, O Lord, and you are exalted as head above all." (1 Chronicles 29:10-11)

King David takes no credit for all the gifts the people have brought to build the temple. He is doing the work of God, on behalf of God. David is the one who gets up early in the morning, stays up late at night, works holidays, makes the deals that need to be made, works with the staff, and all that it takes to run the day to day operations. However, when it comes time to dish out the blessings and the accolades, David gives all honor and praises to God for what is being done. David acknowledges God's ownership and leadership of the building of the Temple and gives God all the credit before the people.

"Riches and honor come from you, and you rule over all. In your hands are power and might; and it is in your hand to make great and to give strength to all" (1 Chronicles 29:12). David knows that the resources: money, people, talent, ideas are in the hand of God. David knows he can only be successful in this building project if he recognizes, acknowledges and leads with God as the true leader. While David is King and has assumed the role of leader, in his heart and mind, God working in and through him leads the way to his success. "And now, our God, we give thanks to you and praise your glorious name" (1 Chronicles 29:13). King David takes the time to give thanks for the works that have been done, for the resources and the people that have participated in and blessed God's enterprise.

"O Lord our God, all this abundance that we have provided for building you a house for your holy name comes from your hand and is all your own" (1 Chronicles 29:16). The resources needed and

69

required for the lavish building of the temple were not just provided, but there was an abundance provided of everything that was needed. David again acknowledges God as the provider and the owner of all that was provided. What a great lesson for all who have the desire to start, own, and run a business successfully.

The moral of the story is if you want to be successful in any business, the riches and honor will come when you acknowledge it as God's business and operate it from your best revelation of divine guidance and wisdom. I love this story because David is surely putting in many hours being King, using his talents to inspire and motivate the people, but by his own admission God is the true business owner and he, David, makes it clear he works for God.

But I cannot end the story until we discuss two additional points that are extremely important to mention here.

"On the next day they offered sacrifices and burnt offerings to the Lord, a thousand bulls a thousand rams, and a thousand lambs, with their libations, and sacrifices in abundance for all Israel; and they ate and drank before the Lord on that day with great joy" (1 Chronicles 29:21).

With this great success story unfolding, there were offerings, celebrations and the pouring of libations. Offerings were made as an outer symbol of thanks to God. In today's terms we would tithe to the place where we get our spiritual nourishment. (And, yes, businesses should tithe from their net profits.)

The celebration was grand and lavish; it was an outer reward for the people who worked diligently toward the success of the business. In today's terms our staff, employees, and volunteers would be acknowledged and appreciated for their efforts.

The pouring of libation was a drink offering most likely of wine. It was made as a sacrifice to God, acknowledging what God had done. In today's terms and in western culture, the pouring of libation would be likened to having a toast at a banquet. Gratitude and thanksgiving would be the sentiment behind the toast. We lift our glasses and speak heart-felt thank you's and affirm continued health, success, prosperity and well-being, all to the glory of God.

"Grant to my son Solomon that with single mind he may keep your commandments, your decrees, and your statutes, performing all of them, and that he may build the temple for which I have made provision....They made David's son Solomon king a second time; they anointed him as the Lord's prince, and Zadok as priest. Then Solomon sat on the throne of the Lord, succeeding his father David as king; he prospered, and all Israel obeyed him. All the leaders and the mighty warriors, and also all the sons of King David, pledged their allegiance to King Solomon. The Lord highly exalted Solomon in the sight of all Israel, and bestowed upon him such royal majesty as had not been on any king before him in Israel" (1 Chronicles 29:22-25).

David was a great example of a divinely guided leader. Then when guided to pass the leadership role to his son, he did everything to prepare Solomon for the position. David prepared Solomon by being an example of a God-centered leader. When the time came Solomon was anointed, meaning a special blessing was conferred upon him, and everyone respected the son because the father had prepared him well.

If our business idea is a divine idea, we want the idea to be carried forth even beyond our tenure. When we start our business we want to be assured that it is such a good idea that it will bless others. We want to see it go forward even when it is time for us to do something different. We truly care about the idea, the source of the idea and those that can be blessed by the idea. We can then make the choice to run and operate the business from this philosophy from day one. We build in our thoughts, early on methods to pass on the blessings of the business.

How may we be in business and be about our Father's business? We keep in mind always that God is the source that is guiding the divine plan of any business venture we could ever enter, and God never fails.

# *Prayer Practice*

Pray about the idea you have for a business until you feel it is indeed a divine idea. Often when ideas come, they need refining through the process of prayer. Ask for guidance and wisdom as you gather your facts and figures and make the necessary inquiries. Use the prayer practices in this book to ground your decision in faith, love, and wisdom.

Often times when people have asked me to bless their business they are talking about the physical space where the business will be located. But as the business owner you should receive the first blessing. You can do the blessing yourself or have your prayer partners or a prayer group that supports you do a special blessing for you.

In that blessing you want to be anointed. Speak words with power to the effect that you are empowered with wisdom and spiritual courage to follow God's guidance; that you are loving in all your interactions with others; and that you always remember God as your source. Affirm that God is the source of the idea for the business and that God is the source of all the abundant prosperity rushing its way to participate in the business named _____.

Take time to sit with the name of the business in your time of meditation. You want the name that is unique and divine for your particular business purpose.

When your physical location is selected (which will be done prayerfully of course), the space itself needs to be blessed.
- Do a space clearing with incense over a 3-day period. For each of the three days, walk through the space gently waving an incense stick (frankincense and myrrh, or sandalwood) with the mental intention to rid the space of any negative energy.
- Burn candles in all rooms. The business owner will have 3 candles lit in his/her space. A white candle representing the spiritual presence of God, a yellow candle representing wisdom, and a purple candle for wealth and spiritual power.

72

- Near the front door burn a green candle for prosperity. If there are other employees, burn candles in their spaces according to the intention you want to set for their particular positions.

Now the space is ready to occupy. Again set your mental intention with every decoration you make and every piece of furniture you place. Have in mind that you are setting up the business to support health, wealth, success and happiness in all that you do.

Now you are ready to have your celebration of friends and supporters to come and bring their positive energy to you, the business, and the space.

This is your public blessing for you and the business. Shape the blessing after King David's example in the form of prayer and ceremony:
- Acknowledge God as the owner and true leader of the enterprise.
- Affirm the idea as a divine idea for which God will provide the necessary resources in abundance.
- Know that as God' living enterprise, you have full access to the inexhaustible supply of riches and honor.
- Commit yourself to be open and receptive to God's guidance in all that you do on behalf of God's business affairs.
- Set the intention to regularly acknowledge God for the success of the business as it does grow and prosper.
- Plan to make regular tithe offerings and do so with the same enthusiasm with which you receive the riches and honor that are sure to come in abundance.

Have someone do a powerful toast (use sparkling cider if you will not use champagne or wine). With God as your partner, well-meaning friends, food, and music added to the celebration, your business will be blessed for grand success.

Many studies have shown that the love and companionship of a dog or cat can be uplifting to one's mental state.

# 10
# Blessing Your Pet

*Prayer Anchor:* "God blessed them, and God said to them, "Be fruitful and multiply, and fill the earth and subdue it; and have dominion over the fish of the sea and over the birds of the air and over every living thing that moves upon the earth" (Genesis 1:28).

From our early beginnings animals have been on the scene and a part of our lives. Our prayer anchor reveals that humankind has a responsibility to care for animals. After all, God blessed every living thing that moves and we should be accountable for the role of dominion we have been entrusted with.

Many of us have pets and they are more than just pets, they are part of the family. We love them, care for them, feed them and certainly they deserve to be blessed just like any other member of the family. Our animals are part of the family not just because we love and care for them but because they in so many ways demonstrate love for us and all the members of the household.

Animals have special lessons that we may learn from them when we are open. Those who have pets in their lives cherish the loving presence of their dog or cat. It is always amazing to watch them and discover the personality that they bring to the household. They affect the very energy of the house with their character.

**Many studies have shown that the love and companionship of a dog or cat can be uplifting to one's mental state.** They seem to have the gift that we humans are working on, unconditional love. Dogs have been called man's best friend for this very reason. Imagine with no capacity to judge others, unconditional love would be easy. And so it is with our pets; they love us with no judgment or criticism, only the desire to be there for us and to be with us.

I always recommend to people who live alone that they should have some other "life giving" energy in their home. Life giving energy is uplifting and helps keep us in tune with growth and stimulates our thoughts of well being. A pet is a great idea if you are willing to take on the responsibility for the care that they need. And yes, pets do require and deserve to be well cared for. Taking on a cat or dog as a pet is likened to the kinds of things we must do when we have a child to care for. So I would carefully make the decision to acquire a pet.

If you're not a dog, cat or bird person, a home can also be blessed by the positive energy of an aquarium filled with thriving fish. And if no animal particularly suits you, live plants in the home can bring in uplifting energy as well.

In the Book of Genesis we are told that humankind has dominion over animals. I believe that dominion means we are responsible for their well being. Dominion gives us the task of stewardship to provide for their needs physically and emotionally. As one creation of God to another, we must do whatever we can to assure that their journey in life is healthy and happy. And what a joy it can be.

## *Prayer Practice*

If you take a pet into your home, make it part of the family. They should have their own space like every member of the household. When you bless the rest of the house, make sure that you bless the space where your pet relaxes and sleeps. Include your pet when you bless the other members of the family. Include a blessing on the meals that you serve him/her.

Those who are not pet owners and lovers may say that you are going overboard, but you have simply taken the charge of "dominion" seriously. You enjoy the love shared between you and your pet, and that is what counts.

Here is a blessing you can say for your pet:

*"Thank you God for the gift of _____(pet's name), I behold him/her as your special creation. I celebrate his/her presence in my*

*life and my presence in his/her life. I bless the closeness we share and this opportunity to participate in loving kindness. Thank You God for _____."*

Say aloud to your beloved pet often:

*"_____(pet's name) you are God's special creation. God's love surrounds you in safety, protection, health and well being, wherever you are, now and always. You are God's blessed gift to me and I am grateful for your presence in my life."*

*Wherever we go,
we want God's
angels helping out
with the details
of the trip.*

# 11
# Travel Safely

*Prayer Anchor:* *"Jacob went on his way and the angels of God met him..." (Genesis 32:1).*

Traveling nowadays can be frustrating, demanding and sometimes out right challenging. But I can think back to when traveling was a bit gentler on the mind and body. I remember the times when I would arrive at the airport just one hour before the flight, check my bag with ease, board the plane in an expedient orderly fashion, be served a full meal with beverage (in coach class), enjoy a movie, land safely, pick up my bag without delay and be out of the airport and on my way. Oh, 'the good old days'.

I remember when I could fill up the gas tank in my 1973 Monte Carlo Chevrolet for just $5. I drove that beautiful gold and black car everywhere. It was nothing to drive out of town for an enjoyable weekend and return home with change in my pocket and the gas tank still a quarter full.

Even before my airplane days and before owning my own car, I once traveled with my mom to Providence, Rhode Island by train from Detroit, Michigan. It was great. Mom and I boarded easily, sat in comfortable seats, ate in the dining car, and enjoyed the beautiful scenery between stops. The journey was long but eventually we arrived at our destination safely.

Today whenever I travel I bless the journey before me. Whenever my children and loved ones travel I bless the journey they take. When I fly, I bless the airplane, the pilots and everyone on board. Whenever I drive, I bless my car. It is comforting for me to bless my travels. It often keeps me from being frustrated when I'm waiting in a long line at the airport, or when I, despite perfect directions, end up driving on the wrong highway 40 miles out of the way.

In 2005 after hurricane Wilma we had difficulty getting gas in Miami and in the surrounding cities. Gas lines were literally miles long. Some folks waited hours in line to get gas in their cars. It was definitely a time when a "travel" blessing was needed. Would it have made the lines move any faster? I don't know, but I do know that the anxiety levels were high, tempers were short, and patience was at an all time low. Peace, harmony, and a spirit of cooperation surely would have helped the stress that many folks expressed in various ways.

When we travel, we want to be like Jacob. We want to have the angels of God meet us on our journey – whether those angels show up in physical form, divine ideas or intuitive messages from within. We want our travels to be blessed with the assurance that we will arrive at our destination safely with few disruptions. We want to be met with experiences that enhance the fun and joy of going new places, meeting new people, or seeing old friends. We want God's angels helping out with the details of every trip we make. We want to experience the difference between a good trip and a great trip. We want to know that we have God's blessings upon all the journeys we make. That's why a travel blessing can help. The details of the trip may or may not be challenging, but you will have the assurance that through it all, you are consciously aware that you are always in God's presence everywhere you go.

I think of the movie "Planes, Trains and Automobiles" starring John Candy and Steve Martin. In the movie, what started out to be a normal business trip turned into a traveler's nightmare. Nothing seemed to go their way no matter how they traveled - by plane, train, or automobile. By the end of the movie, what appeared to be a chance meeting between these two men, joined together by a series of travel disasters, turned out to be the beginning of a new friendship.

Even if we make all the preparations, do all the blessings we know, what appears to be the worst trip in terms of travel mishaps can still turn out to be a gift we hadn't expected. Your trip will be so much more enjoyable with conscious intention to remain calm through any delays, miscommunications, and detours. If you can be at peace within, the outer journey will follow your lead. And who knows as you travel what angels you'll meet in the process, or what wonderful gifts await you on the pathway to your destination.

When you bless your travels in advance, you are praying up the entire experience. You set an intention that your trip will be blessed and that angels of God will meet you on your way. However, I have discovered that much of my own travel success is greatly improved when I have done my part in preparing for the journey. Just the little things like taking the car in for a check up before driving on a long trip, or making sure to keep my valuables with me when I travel by plane, or making sure my passport is in order well in advance of my international voyages can make a big difference in my experience.

Blessing your trip with a prayer is no substitute for doing your part in planning and preparation. For a blessed trip, plan carefully, bless your journey with prayer, set your intention for a safe and successful trip, and then go expecting to meet angels of God on the journey.

## _Prayer Practice_

Again, take the time to plan your trip in detail, from what to pack, checking the weather, having adequate directions, making sure you have proper identification, to securing your credit cards, etc. Do not underestimate your ability to make your travels successful by doing your part with the details.

Once you've done your part with the preparation, it is time to bless your journey.

- Before your leave your home, bless your home with a brief prayer. Make your own statement, but here is a simple example: "I am grateful that this house is divinely protected in my absence. The peaceful presence and power of God watches over this home day and night." Short, simple and to the point. You may not think this so important, but during one of the many hurricane warnings we had one year, I blessed my home and left before the hurricane hit our area. As I was driving back to the area 4 days later I did not know what shape my home would be in. The reports were that a lot

85

of damage had been done to the area with few people having electricity. When I arrived home, my home had a few tiles missing from my roof and my fence that had already been in disrepair was down. Several of my neighbors had a lot more damage than I did. And, my neighborhood was one of the few that had electricity. From the appearance of my items in the refrigerator, I had only lost electrical power for a short time. There were neighborhoods in Miami that did not have electricity for a month. Bless your home before you leave it to set in your mind that it is divinely protected.

- Say a prayer of blessing for yourself before you walk out of your door saying something like: "God's presence goes before me making my journey safe, smooth, and successful in every way. I travel under the grace of God and only good can meet me on this journey." If others are traveling with you, have them join you in the prayer.

- If you are traveling by plane or train. It is important to bless the vehicle once you are on it. Say a prayer to the effect: "God's loving presence surrounds this _____(airplane, train, bus, etc), and every person on it. God is directing the _____(pilot, conductor, bus driver, etc) with divine wisdom and right choices. We travel with ease and under grace arriving safely at our destination."

- When you are ready to return home from your trip, again, say a blessing for you and anyone who is traveling with you. Of course bless the mode of transportation that brings you safely back home just as you did before.

- When you arrive back at home, give thanks that all is well. "I am grateful to know that all is well with my home. The peaceful presence and power of God continues to watch over this home day and night." I (we) live in this home protected always by the grace of God.

As you travel, depend on God's presence no matter the circumstances surrounding your journey. Take every opportunity to bless your travels with a prayer of guidance, wisdom, protection, safety and then add some joy and fun to it.

*You receive according to the level of generosity that you mirror in your experiences of giving.*

# 12
## Claim Your Overflowing Blessings

*Prayer Anchor: "Bring the full tithe into the storehouse, so that there may be food in my house, and thus put me to the test, says the Lord of hosts; see if I will not open the windows of heaven for you and pour down for you an overflowing blessing" (Malachi 3:10).*

Now what does tithing have to do with prayer? Everything. Just as prayer is an act of faith, so is tithing. When we pray, we acknowledge God as the source from which we faithfully expect our answers to come. When we tithe, we acknowledge that God is the source of what we have already received, as well as the inexhaustible supply from which more is to come.

Tithing is a prayer in and of itself. It is a prayer of gratitude, celebration and joyful expectation for continued blessings. When we give 10% of our income from all channels to the place that represents God – usually a religious or spiritual organization, we are responding to the gifts God has already provided for us. At the same time we are making a spiritual investment toward future blessings that are sure to follow.

When we were children our parents taught us that when someone gives us something we should say "thank you." When we tithe it is a form of saying and expressing a sincere thank you to God for what we have received. The expression of our gratitude aligns us with a consciousness to subsequently attain even more.

The prayer anchor for this chapter tells us to try tithing. The promise is that we will be rewarded with overflowing blessings for our faithful actions. Before I put God to the test – this test of tithing that is, I used to think that tithing was something that preachers made up to coerce people to give money to the church. I didn't have much money in those days and really didn't see any purpose in giving it to the church. I felt like I needed my money more that the church did.

The preacher surely made a higher income than I did, so it stood to reason in my mind that when the preacher started talking about tithing he was talking to the other folks in church, not to me.

It was not until I found myself in the place where my life was in such bad shape that I was finally willing to at least listen to the tithing message. I had reached the place I call "back up against the wall." My health, relationships and finances were all failing and I was desperate to consider possibilities I would not have previously considered - yes, even tithing.

I decided to take the scripture to heart. I read it over and over again, just to make sure I understood it. The more I read, the more interested I became to see just what God could do in my life. I, skeptically, chose to try it. I really didn't think it would work for me, but I had run out of things to try. For weeks I put myself through an inner struggle trying to decide if tithing would work for me or not. I finally came to a decision: I wanted the "windows of heaven to pour down for me an overflowing blessing."

So I tried it. When the offering basket came around on Sunday, I held the envelope tightly; it was as if I was giving up everything I owned in that moment. At the time, it was a tremendous leap of faith to give 10% of my income, particular when I was working hard to make the 100% cover my living expenses. Holding my tithe, I recited the offering blessing along with the other givers. By this time I had memorized Malachi 3:10, so, still holding the envelope tightly, I recited it to myself. I needed the assurance that I could expect my "overflowing blessing."

I continued to read Malachi 3:10 and give my tithe each week. The prayer seemed to work. Tithing seemed to work. Things got better in my life for a while. But once things got better, I stopped reading Malachi 3:10. I stopped tithing. Somehow I had fallen into the error thought that I had received my overflowing blessing and I would just keep receiving even after I had stopped giving. Over time, things got increasingly worse.

It took several years of tithing off and on until I made a conscious whole-hearted commitment to regular prayer and tithing. Like many folks I loved to receive but giving had somehow eluded my understanding as being an affirmation of gratitude for answered prayer, and the many blessings in my life. I had not connected tithing with my faith in God and the promises revealed to the prophet Malachi thousands of years ago. I had no problem asking God for what I needed, but I didn't think that giving had much to do with my receiving. It took years but I did eventually get Jesus' message: "give, and it will be given to you. A good measure, pressed down, shaken together, running over, will be put into your lap; for the measure you give will be the measure you get back" (Luke 6:38-39).

I am proud to tell you today (and now for many years) I have been committed to tithing. I understand now that if I want to receive then I must demonstrate a giving consciousness. Today, I enjoy giving as a demonstration of my faith and gratitude for all that I can be, have, and do. And now that I am a minister, I teach it, not to coerce others to give to the church but because I want to see others claim their overflowing blessings.

Well, I will be the first to tell you that if you are not willing to learn the lessons that are inherent in generous, unconditional, anxiety-free giving, then tithing is a bitter pill to swallow. So let me give you the tools that will help you understand the basics of tithing and support you in becoming a consistent, happy tither.

What is a tithe?

We first see tithing in the Bible in Genesis 14 where Abram gives a tenth of all that he collected from the spoils of a battle to Melchizedek who was a "priest of God Most High" (Genesis 14:18).

Ten percent of all the income you receive from all channels is given with love and gratitude to the place where you get your spiritual nourishment. And you should be getting spiritual nourishment from somewhere. We must also tithe our time and spiritual gifts. When we give our attention to studying, learning, reading, praying, meditating, we are giving back to God from the time we have been given. Tithing of our spiritual gifts of talents means we find a place to be of service. Whatever abilities we have to give in service, we express our gratitude by helping others with the abilities God has given us.

Where to give your tithe:

In tithing to a church you must ask yourself "do I believe and trust that this church represents God, God's work, God's purposes for the lives of the people who attend, and for the people it serves?" Whether you tithe your time, spiritual gifts or money, you should feel that the place where your give your tithe represents high spiritual ideals through its works, deeds, and teachings. If you tithe to an individual your questioning should be the same. If so, then that is where you want to tithe. The place where you tithe should be the place where you are continually reminded and involved in God's purposes of love, peace, truth, and prosperity.

Why tithe?

The bigger more important question is: Do you want the "windows of heaven to pour down for you an overflowing blessing?" Giving and receiving represents two sides of the same spiritual law. If we receive we must complete the transaction by giving. And as we give, we set a cycle of activity in motion - that of giving and receiving. The more we give, the more we can expect to receive, and a continuous flow of giving and receiving keeps our good circulating.

When to tithe:

As soon as you have something to tithe on: time, spiritual gifts and/or money, that's when you tithe. When you wake up in the morning and realize you have been blessed with another day, immediately tithe some of your time in prayer, meditation, or some kind of spiritual devotional activity. Accept opportunities to be of service in your community or with your spiritual community. This is tithing your talents or spiritual gifts.

If you receive your income weekly, tithe weekly, if money comes to you monthly, tithe monthly. If you receive an unexpected money gift (and if you are a tither, you will receive unexpected money blessings), write your tithe check then or set the money apart to give it at your next opportunity. Some folks mail tithes to the church as soon as they write the check so that they are sure they keep their good circulating.

Tithing is a practice that expands the generosity of your spirit. When you are a generous person, you draw to you the generosity of others toward you. **You receive according to the level of generosity that you mirror in your experiences of giving.**

## *Prayer Practice*

If you are already a tither, then you already know the value of giving to God's work. Long time tithers discover that tithing trains us to be good spiritual givers in all areas of life. That is, giving becomes not so much our tithe, but a way of life. Most of the tithers I know give well above and beyond 10% of income and are very active in serving others. Tithers are usually dedicated to their prayer life and the study of Truth; it's what keeps them actively living the principle of giving and receiving. Keep yourself grounded in faith in God and continue to express your gratitude in as many ways as you can. I do suggest that you take the time to read Chapters Malachi 3 and 4. Make a study of its metaphysical meaning. Your commitment to God will only deepen.

If you are not a tither, you may need some mental and emotional conditioning before you start to tithe financially. Read the prayer anchor for this chapter 3 times a day for 21 days. Don't just the read the scripture however, attempt to understand the message being conveyed through Malachi's revelation from God. *During the 21-day period, pray to have your consciousness of generosity opened to a new level so that you may give unconditionally, regularly, and from a consciousness of faith and thanksgiving.*

If you are grateful for what God has and is doing in your life, then let your giving reflect it. I never suggest that people begin attempting to tithe with 2% or anything less than 10%. Why? The word tithe means a tenth. There is no such thing as a partial tithe. Tithing is an act of faith.  If we do not put God to the full test we are not putting our faith in God and we are putting our trust in our circumstances.  So if you're not ready to tithe, just keep giving at your current level until you have reached a level of faith where you are willing to take God's challenge whole heartedly.  There are many books on tithing and stewardship programs in many churches to help you embrace tithing with joy.

Find a place to volunteer your spiritual gifts or talents.  If you are not ready to begin financial tithing, you can always start here and add on financial tithing when you are ready.  But do plan to tithe of time, spiritual gifts and finances.  It all works together and constitutes full giving of the tithe.

Make it a practice to pray daily.  That is the theme of this book.  No matter what prayer you pray or what scripture you read the more time you spend with your mind and heart centered in God, the more you access your divine ability to live the quality of life that you deserve and desire.  As you open your mind to a greater awareness of giving in all areas:  time, service and finances, your receiving consciousness will surely grow.  Living from this new level of consciousness, you claim your overflowing blessings.

Do not wait until a
health challenge arises
to speak loving words
to your body.

# 13
## *Pleasant Words, Healthy Body*

***Prayer Anchor:*** *"Pleasant words are like a honeycomb, sweetness to the soul and health to the body" (Proverbs 16:24).*

As spiritual beings dressed in a physical body, we are responsible to maintain the outfit we're wearing. But our Creator has truly blessed us by equipping us with spiritual and mental tools for this sometimes seemingly awesome task. When we use the spiritual and mental tools at our disposal, we can really do a good job of taking excellent care of the suit that covers our soul.

For example, we have our spiritual tools of prayer and meditation. Then we have our mental tools of life-affirming thoughts and words. And then there is the gift of having our minds and bodies so carefully and wisely designed that they respond to the spiritual and mental tools when we use them. When we combine these tools, toward the goal of personal bodily self care, we can benefit all three aspects of our being - spirit, mind, and body - at the same time. As we apply the practices of prayer and meditation with life-affirming thoughts and words, we initiate the best health care plan a body could possibly have.

Our successful personal health care plan can work like this: When we pray and meditate, we condition our thoughts. Thoughts shape ideas, and ideas come alive through our words. Words are like missionaries going out to fulfill the purpose for which they are spoken. "So shall my word be that goes out from my mouth; it shall not return to me empty, but it shall accomplish that which I purpose, and succeed in the thing for which I sent it" (Isaiah 55:11). We can then use the power of our words as an important foundation for good mental and physical health.

Words reveal the thoughts that we think, and together they shape our experiences. When we think of ourselves as healthy, the words we send forth help to shape healthy experiences just as we have verbalized it. Since we have the God-given ability to create our experiences, we use our thoughts and our words as activators for what we desire to create. So if we're going to be creating anyway, we may as well create what we want rather than what we do not want. It just makes good sense to make it a goal and set an intention to create a healthy body while speaking the words of a healthy mind.

Some of the ways we can use our words to create and support a healthy mind and body are speaking words that bless, affirm life, and recognize only wholeness. Myrtle Fillmore, cofounder of Unity, spoke words of health and praise to her body and was healed of what she was told was a terminal illness. If you would like more information on her healing, Unity[1] publishes a pamphlet "How I found Health" by Myrtle Fillmore. We too can use our words, backed by the power of a prayer-filled consciousness of health, to bring about healing of every kind. We should do this when we are experiencing a health challenge, but also when we are not. **Do not wait until a health challenge arises to speak loving words to your body.** When you speak words that affirm health to your body, the body benefits and your mind receives nourishment also.

## *Prayer Practice*

In your time of prayer, speak affirmative words about your mind and to your body. Speak to every area of your body from the top of your head to the soles of your feet. Visualize yourself healthy in mind, body, and affairs as you speak the words.

Here are some examples, but do form your own; they will have more meaning and power for you if you create them especially for your use and enjoyment:

Focusing your attention on your eyes, say to your eyes: *"You see clearly without strain. You are the perfect set of eyes for me and I bless all that you do for me. You see good everywhere and in all*

---

[1] Unity School of Christianity is located in Unity Village, Missouri 64065

*people. I love you and appreciate you for helping me see life, love, wisdom, and truth in all my experiences."*

Focusing your attention on your heart, say to your heart: *"Thank you for being a radiating center of love. Thank you for beating the appropriate number of times each moment of my days. Thank you for pumping blood easily through my veins. I bless you as a healthy organ in my body fulfilling the divine purpose for which God appointed you."*

Focusing inward for your overall health and well-being: *"I am grateful for my healthy, attractive, vibrant body. Every cell in my body is healthy, well, blessed, and radiant. I enjoy my body, and my body enjoys me. Good health is mine now and always."*

Focusing your attention on the area between your eyes (the third eye) or at the very top of your head (crown chakra): *"My mind is in tune with the mind of God. I think clearly, I know what is mine to know. I understand easily, and when divinely inspired, take appropriate spirit-guided action. Spirit flows in and through my whole thinking process with wisdom, power, and ease. My thoughts are programmed for positive ideas and grand success."*

As you prayerfully affirm positive statements to bless your mind and body, you'll develop the habit of saying kind things about you, to you. This will also facilitate being kind to your mind and body in outer ways through positive healthful lifestyle choices.

*Through our prayers, we will discover that our connection with our loved one is not lost but altered toward spiritual understanding, growth, and wholeness.*

## 14
## *When a Loved one Dies*

*Prayer Anchor:* *"Yeah though I walk through the valley of the shadow of death I will fear no evil for thou art with me; thy rod and thy staff they comfort me....Surely goodness and mercy shall follow me all the days of my life and I will dwell in the house of the Lord forever" (Psalm 23:4,6 KJV).*

When a loved one leaves our physical presence by way of the transition we call death, we wonder about the experience of death itself and what it means. We have many questions. We wish there was something we could do to rest assured that our loved one is not somewhere hurting, missing us as we are missing them. We want to get through our own thoughts of fear and sometimes guilt. We want the pain of loss and separation to subside. We want to know if our loved one is somehow OK in spite of the grief we are feeling.

The scripture from the 23<sup>rd</sup> Psalm is often read at funerals and memorial services. The entire scripture is a powerful prayer that has instilled hope, comfort, and promise in the human heart and mind for thousands of years. It is probably one of the most popular scriptures in the Old Testament of the Bible. We can pray it on behalf of our loved ones to gain reassurance that they are not alone or afraid. We can pray this prayer to begin our own healing journey through the difficult process we know as grief.

Two verses in the scripture can be particularly comforting to mourning family and friends. Verse 4 can be read to tell us our loved one walked through the valley of the very shadow of death and was not afraid of the experience called death. This addresses one of the concerns we have about death, does it hurt? Should we be afraid of the experience? If we believe the powerful words of this scripture the answers would be no and no. We can take some comfort in believing that our loved one crossed death's door and did so with such peace that there was no pain and no fear.

The second part of verse 4 addresses our concern for the location of our loved one. Where did they go when they left our sight? Where are they now? The Psalmist assures us that wherever we are God is with us and we are with God. Not only is God with our loved one but they are comforted by God's loving presence, the rod and staff of love and peace. Whatever plane of existence our loved one has moved on to, they are not in pain, not afraid, they are with God and comforted with love and peace all about them.

Verse 6 tells us "goodness and mercy will follow us all the days of our lives." The question for some of us then is: "but what about life after death?" Does the goodness and mercy follow us after all the days of what we call our life? Is death the absence of life? Or is it a continuation of life but in a different form? These are the kinds of questions we will find our answers to according to our religious or spiritual beliefs.

I believe it is natural to bring up the question of eternal life when we are concerned about the fate of our dearly departed loved one. My purpose here is not to convince anyone that life is eternal. I however suggest that since the transition we call death is something we will all face at some point, it may be healing to at least consider it as a possibility for and on behalf of our loved one, and hope it is true for ourselves.

Verse 6 ends this powerful prayer: "And I will dwell in the house of the Lord forever." Since our loved one is not with us physically, it may be comforting to know their location is in the house of the Lord, which we may feel is the next best thing if they are not physically with us.

I believe that it is healthy to have questions about life and death, death and dying, birth and eternal life. I've not tried to answer those questions here for you, only to stir up your beliefs for possible confirmation, reconsideration or more in-depth study.

106

I do believe we owe it to our departed loved one to hold in our minds the best possible thoughts we can toward the experience on their behalf. And, on their behalf, take some time to send our love and blessings through the process of prayer to them in whatever form they have taken in their next experience of existence. We can fill that void in our hearts that wants to do something by praying for them this powerful prayer from the 23rd Psalm.

In the process we will learn what is ours to know from this side of the experience. **Through our prayers, we will discover that our connection with our loved one is not lost but altered toward spiritual understanding, growth, and wholeness.** As we heal through our own grief, we gain the insight that love "...bears all things, believes all things, hopes all things, endures all things. Love never ends." (1 Corinthians 13:7, 8).

Our feelings cause us to want to do something toward our own assurance that our loved one is somehow all right. We can do this through prayer. At the same time we are praying for the well being of our loved one, we are also setting in motion a healthy intention for us to heal and let go that part of our relationship that is finished.

## *Prayer Practice*

As soon after the transition is made or as the person is making their transition, light a white candle on their behalf. If you have a picture of the person you may place the candle near the picture. Begin to pray. Speak the person's name and give thanks to God for a peaceful transition, a healing transition, a spiritual walk into the light of everlasting divine love. Envision a white light surrounding the person as healing light. Know that on the soul level, whatever healing needs to take place is done.

Pray the 23$^{rd}$ Psalm on behalf of your loved one in this way:

*"Dear _____(name of the person), The Lord God is your shepherd you shall never again want for anything.*

*You now rest in green pastures of eternal love. You are guided on a journey near the still waters of perfect peace, and your soul is restored to wholeness.*

*You walk in right paths of pure knowing for the sake of the one presence and power now confirmed to you as God within and all around you.*

*Even though you walk through what you once believed was a dark valley called death, you have no fear, now you walk in the light of Truth.*

*You feel the rod and staff of love and peace upon your spirit, and discover the comfort of true eternal bliss.*

*You find a banquet table of all good laid out before you in the place where there is no knowledge of, or idea called an enemy. Your head is anointed with sweet fragrances of various healing oils, and now you know true prosperity.*

*Dear _____(name of the person) I rejoice with you for the goodness and mercy that enfolds you now and throughout eternity. I find my own personal joy and comfort in knowing you dwell in the consciousness of eternal love now and forever. Amen!"*

Light a candle and pray this prayer once a day for nine days. Know that as you pray this prayer for your loved one, you are also beginning your healing process.

If at no other time you can think of when you need a spiritual community, it is especially important when mourning the loss of a loved one. In my experience the people whose lives are devastated to the point of slow, or no return, are those who did not have a spiritual support system to help them grieve healthily. Spiritual counseling, support groups and prayer are the tools we need to help us move through the grief process with poise and grace. My suggestion: Don't attempt to go through grief alone, get help and let others pray with you and for you.

# Part Three


# Prayer Practices That add energy and power

We should not underestimate any of our God given senses. They have the ability to change our emotional state in a moment.

# 15
## The Sweet Smell of Answered Prayer

*Prayer Anchor:* *"Then Noah built an ark to the Lord, and took of every clean animal and of every clean bird, and offered burnt offerings on the altar. And when the Lord smelled the pleasing odor, the Lord said in his heart, 'I will never again curse the ground because of humankind'... "* *(Genesis: 8:20-21).*

In ancient times scented oils and fragrant materials were used during religious rituals. There was a belief that the fragrance would attract the attention of God, and their prayer would be favored because of the sweet smell. The Egyptians were reported to be very fond of aromatic substances and used them often and generously. These oils were also used to adorn the body in various kinds of rituals and ceremonies as well. They believed it, and they made fragrances a part of their religious practices.

Aromatherapy as we know it today is the evolution of some early beliefs that there was a connection between scent and health, scent and beauty, scent and sensuality, scent and certain states of consciousness. I'm sure you have certain scents that evoke certain states of being within you.

For a time, when I was a young girl I lived with my oldest sister, her husband and their three children. My father died when I was four years old and living with my sister was the first time I'd really felt part of a family where there was a dad present. Every morning my sister would make her husband breakfast and send him off to work at about 5:00 a.m. So I would wake up to the aroma of coffee, bacon, homemade bread and sometimes apple cinnamon rolls.

Well, even today some 40 years later (and although I don't drink coffee or eat bacon or apple cinnamon rolls), when I smell any of the three or all three, it brings a smile to my face in memory of some very happy childhood times. The smell takes me back 40 years, and causes me to smile.

Our sense of smell can trigger memories, feelings and emotions as well as prepare the mind for clarity. **We should not underestimate any of our God-given senses. They have the ability to change our emotional state in a moment.** Think about it for a moment, does any particular smell take you back to a happy time or even a sad time?

The above scripture illustrated God as changing his heart by smelling a pleasing odor, but it is you and I whose minds may be opened up and changed by taking in fragrant aromas.

Certain scents are said to be effective in addressing certain complaints, whether they be mental, physical, or emotional. They can also be used simply for lifting our spirit. If you are interested in aromatherapy, I would recommend that you do some study on your own and then talk to an aromatherapy practitioner. Unless you are addressing an illness, I suggest you use your own nose as your guide. Trying essential oils that are pleasing to you is the best place to start, in addition to reading up on the subject.

Here are a few suggestions when using essential oils. Look for good quality oil. Check the label for "pure essential oil." Before applying oil to a large area of your skin, or using in your bath water, test the oil first with just a drop to assure that the oil is compatible with your skin.

There are varieties of ways to use scented oils. You may use essential oils on your body; inhale the fragrance directly from the bottle; put a few drops in a diffuser or air freshener; add a few drops to your bath water, or try any other uses that may come to you.

Here are some of the common scents used: lavender, peppermint, jasmine, rose and frankincense. If you are not familiar with aromatherapy, I recommend getting a nice diffuser to start with and begin with a few drops of lavender. Let yourself enjoy the aromatic fragrance. If you have a very sensitive sense of smell, start slow and

114

in small portions with the oils that you select. You may want to experiment with many fragrances before settling on a few that work well for you.

## *Prayer Practice*

Select a scent that is pleasing to you. Look into the different uses for specific oils to see if there is a fragrance that relates to a particular prayer request that you have. For example, if you were feeling stressed, tired, maybe even worried put a few drops of lavender in your diffuser, place it within the range of your smell and then spend some time in silent prayer. If you really want to relax, run yourself a warm bath, put a few drops of lavender in your bath water, light a lavender-scented candle and enjoy your silent prayer from your tub. (Again, always test an oil before using it in your bath. Try a drop on your skin just to make sure it is not irritable to you).

If you're praying for a right and perfect mate, you might use rose or jasmine scents in your diffuser to lift your receptivity to love. If you want to let your mind flow into a deep meditation, frankincense would be a great support for this. Use lavender and peppermint scents for relaxation. Again, your nose is your best judge, along with a little bit of study. Try many scents until you hit on a few that you really like.

As always, set your intention as you are putting your diffuser in place and setting your oil in it. To be most effective, know your desire before using this spiritual practice as with any others that are mentioned in this book.

When you pray, let your sense of smell support you as you breathe deeply for a few minutes. Center your thoughts on the presence of God within. Always remember that the aroma can support your physical and emotional concentration as you prayer; it is not a substitute for prayer. Begin your prayer and enjoy the sweet smell of answered prayer.

*Sacred symbols
and objects rightly used
can help us focus on God's
presence within.*

# 16
## Prayer and Sacred Symbols

*Prayer Anchor: "Then the priests brought the ark of the covenant of the Lord to its place, in the inner sanctuary of the house, in the most holy place, underneath the wings of the cherubim. For the cherubim spread out their wings over the place of the ark, so that the cherubim made a covering above the ark and its poles"*
*(1 Kings 8:6, 7).*

The Ark of the Covenant was Israel's most sacred religious artifact. The above scripture reveals that it was precious and treated with reverence. It was placed in "the most holy place" within the sanctuary and underneath the wings of angels as a protective covering.

The religious practice of having a sacred and holy place specifically set aside for acknowledging God's presence, has been handed down to us over the ages. It has given rise to many folks setting up an altar in their homes with personal sacred objects that remind them of God's presence.

Most religions and cultures have their own sacred symbols that have particular meaning and purpose to them. If you were to walk in the home of a person today, you might see some of those sacred symbols displayed as angels, a picture of Jesus, a crucifix, a picture of the Virgin Mary, a statue of Buddha, etc.

These symbols have their unique meaning to one's culture or religion but have meaning on an individual level as well. For this reason, if you are guided to have an altar in your home, you would select the symbols to be placed on that altar according to your own beliefs regarding any objects that you place upon it. Each item on your altar should have personal significance to you. This is an important key to

119

your empowerment when you pray before your altar or when you pray using the sacred symbols from your altar.

Our ideas about what is sacred in our religious and spiritual practices stem from what we learned from our ancestors. As we took charge of our own spiritual education, we gained expanded spiritual knowledge.

Trust yourself with regard to what speaks to you and why. When you select sacred objects to use in your prayer practices, they should have meaning to you and a purpose for which you use them.

Use caution, however. There is a danger of having an altar and using sacred objects in our prayer practices. Many battles ended with the winner taking possession of the Ark away from Israel. Many lives were sacrificed to re-capture the Ark and get it back to Jerusalem.

That same danger exists for us. Although we may not literally lose our lives over our sacred objects, we can lose our power by freely giving it up to an object we think we need to feel God's presence. There is always the danger of putting our faith in the object. We may fall into the trap of putting our hope in an object. When we are separated from it, we may have difficulty becoming consciously aware of God's presence within. We can find ourselves making a statue of Jesus or the Virgin Mary that which we worship. That is a form of losing ourselves and our spiritual stronghold on Truth.

So, while I do say it is an acceptable and helpful practice to have an altar, place specifically selected sacred symbols upon it, and even use those symbols in your prayer time. Remember to keep yourself balanced with their use and meaning as part of your spiritual practice. Let your devotion be to your higher power-God in you.

**Sacred symbols and objects rightly used can help us focus on God's presence within.** We can use them as a means of drawing from our own spiritual and religious beliefs. What we think and feel regarding the objects can support us in feeling God's presence within. The use of sacred symbols and objects can best support our prayer practices when we remember that they are symbols that we may use to acknowledge a much deeper power that is within us.

120

Anything you do on the outer, has already been done by you on the inner. So if you choose not to set up an altar for prayer and meditation in your home, set one up in your own mind and visit there on a regular basis. This way wherever you go you take your altar with you.

If you do decide to set up a physical altar in your home, get clear on your purpose for having it and why it is important for you. Always use your spiritual understanding to discern what is right for you.

Arrange your altar in a place that is not on public display or in view of anyone who enters your home. If someone does see your altar, it should be because you have specifically invited him or her to do so. Each person's energy is different according to their beliefs, and their beliefs may not be in harmony with yours. "But whenever you pray go into your room and shut the door and pray to your Father who is in secret and your Father who sees in secret will reward you" (Matthew 6:6).

You may want to look into the Chinese art of Feng Shui, which is the ancient philosophy of right placement to maximize the flow of energy in our environment. Using the Feng Shui principles, you'll be able to determine which area of your home will be most conducive to prayerful, peaceful meditative energy. You may also use the principles of Feng Shui to help with where to locate items on your altar.

Here are a few general suggestions for your altar, however, let your intuition guide you in what has a right feeling for you. You are always your own best guide as to what is best for you. You may use the trial and error method as well, try what you feel may be right and notice what happens as a result. As you pay attention to your life, you will be able to determine if you are on the right track.

Select items carefully to be placed on your altar. They should speak to your personal spiritual beliefs. Do not crowd your altar. More doesn't necessarily mean better. Keep your altar clean; remember it is a place for sacred symbols, items such as candles, incense and aromatherapy diffuser, if you are into essential oils. Don't be afraid to add color; white is the color that most often represents spirituality, purification and healing, but here again be guided from within. Then, place your sacred objects on the altar, which may include your statues of goddesses, saints, personal heroes and sheroes and whatever feels right to you. It would also be appropriate to place your stones, crystals, etc. as you like them. The important thing is that each item you place is for a purpose and has meaning for you.

## Prayer Practice

If you choose to set up an altar, make it personal with your preferences and spiritual practices. Let yourself be of the consciousness that your true altar is within. You may still choose to have a physical place in the outer with material objects to support your inner work.

Your altar should be a place where you feel drawn to pray, meditate, sit in the silence, and have your regular devotional experience. The more you pray up the space, the deeper your experience will be at your altar. Whether you decide to kneel, sit, or stand is your preference, but a consistent habit of prayer at your altar will strengthen the energetic vibration you experience while praying there. You may be guided to hold an object from your altar during your prayer time. This is perfectly fine, just remember that you are not putting your power in the object but you are open to the energy of being in a positive energy flow with whatever item you hold. God in you is the power.

Your altar and your prayer practices before your altar are personal to your spiritual and religious beliefs. Enjoy the space you have created to acknowledge, honor, and celebrate your relationship with God's presence in you.

We light a candle and enjoy its beauty, embrace its fragrance and celebrate the flame it mirrors in us.

# 17
## Light a Candle

*Prayer Anchor: "Take heed therefore that the light which is in thee be not darkness. If thy whole body therefore be full of light, having no part dark, the whole shall be full of light, as when the bright shining of a candle doth give thee light" (Luke 11:35-36; KJV).*

When we light a candle for the purpose of setting our intention toward prayer, we are reminded that the light of truth the spark of divinity is within us. We light the candle to enhance our inner light. If there is any darkness in us (meaning negativity, fear, or worry), turning on the light will chase the darkness away. Lighting an outer candle can be an inner affirmation that we do not choose to carry darkness or negativity into our time of prayer. As we turn our thoughts to the outer light, all our inner error beliefs are brought into the light of life, love, wisdom, and truth. We symbolically turn on our inner light when we light a candle.

As I have said several times in this book, we never put our faith in outer symbols but we may use them to enhance our ability to focus inward. **We light a candle and enjoy its beauty, embrace its fragrance, and celebrate the flame it mirrors in us.** The flame reflects the light of truth within us and supports us on our inward journey.

The time will come in our spiritual unfoldment when the outer candle is no longer necessary or desired. We will be in the spiritual space that John speaks of: "And there shall be no night there; and they need no candle, neither light of the sun; for the Lord God giveth them light; and they shall reign for ever and ever" (Revelations 22:5).

But as we are on the journey of spiritual evolution, we may light a candle as we are building a consciousness that is fully aware of the inner light, reflected by an outer light. So, if you enjoy burning candles as part of your spiritual practice, do so with an understanding of its purpose for you and your spiritual growth.

Candles can be scented, if we choose to engage our sense of smell. Candles come in all kinds of beautiful shapes and sizes, so we may also engage our physical sight while we enjoy the striking glow of a lit candle.

Then there is color. There are all kinds of theories on the effect that color may have on our emotional state, health, attitudes, etc. There are many books written on the subject for more information on what color of candle is best for you to burn and when to use particular colors.

Here are a few very general guidelines on selection of candles to use for your spiritual practices.

## Color Preferences

Burn:

- Red to incite passion, it evokes feelings of love, invigorates healing energy. This color is said to be so stimulating that it may increase the heart rate and may have a good effect on people with low blood pressure.
- Orange as an attention getter. Its vibration is to draw energy to it: ideas, romance, money, beauty, encouragement, friendship.
- Yellow for inner joy, feelings of happiness, vitality, inspiration, illumination, mental stimulation.
- Green for health, tranquility, sense of meaning and purpose, prosperity.
- Blue for inner peace, relaxation. It is said to enhance our faith, hope, expectation of good.
- Purple for the feeling of wealth, prosperity, royalty, power, sensuality, spirituality.

- Pink for relaxation, calmness, drawing on inner beauty; evokes feelings of love (for self, life, God, and others), intimacy, and romance.
- White as it brings forth clarity, purity and spiritual power.

## Number of Candles to Burn

How many candles to burn at a time? Use your own intuition on this, but be aware that certain numbers of candles may support your purpose more so than others. In the study of numerology, certain numbers carry a vibration and energy that affects us just as does color, shape, and type of candle does. *See the section at the beginning of the book titled "How to Use This Book" for some additional discussion on numbers.*

## Shapes to Consider

Candles come in many shapes that represent a particular symbolism. You may have seen crucifix candles, or candles in the shape of a man or woman, heart shaped candles; you name it; there is great variety available. I suggest that if burning candles is a regular part of your spiritual practice you will enjoy experimenting with various selections of candles.

Personally I burn candles almost daily in my spiritual practices. I like color, fragrance, the warm glow of the flame and the symbolism of reflecting my inner light. I find that the tea light candles are convenient, cost-effective, safe and available in a variety of colors, so this works for me. I use longer burning candles for various purposes. For example, as I spend this day writing, I am burning a heart-shaped pink candle. In my prayer time this morning, I set an intention to be open to the relaxed, soothing, calming effects of divine love in me as I enjoy this day of writing.

## *Prayer Practice*

Decide on your purpose for using a candle in your prayer practice. This will help you select the color, shape, size, and number of candles to burn. Remember to take safety precautions whenever you burn candles.

When you light your candle mentally set an intention lighting each candle. Often, when I perform a wedding ceremony, the couples will elect to light two small tapered candles and jointly light one large candle. The outer representation is that the two people join their lives together as one.

Light your candle, and begin your prayer. Let the outer light be a reminder of your own inner light that is waiting to express in and through you in an infinite number of ways. "You are the light of the world" (Matthew 5:14).

*There is a*
*rhythmic celebration going*
*on inside us all the time.*

# 18
## Add Soul-Stirring Music

*Prayer Anchor:* "*Praise him with trumpet sound; praise him with lute and harp! Praise him with tambourine and dance; praise him with strings and pipe! Praise him with clanging cymbals; praise him with loud clashing cymbals! Let everything that breathes praise the Lord! Praise the Lord" (Psalm 150:3-6)!*

Did you ever hear a piece of music that brought you to tears? Perhaps you've heard a piece of music that emotionally affected you and you felt sad or happy or it caused you to want to dance or clap. Perhaps you've heard music that took you to another place mentally and you thought about the past, future, or things imagined.

Music has the ability to reach deep places within us even when words cannot. Life itself has a compelling rhythm and our hearts beat to it. **There is a rhythmic celebration going on inside us all the time.** The tune is set to the cadence of life that performs within us in sweet harmonic communion with God every moment.

Add music to your personal prayer practice from time to time. Seek out various kinds of music that connect with your emotional state. I won't recommend any specific pieces or artists, but there are many for you to choose from. Searching for the music that stirs your soul will be an added blessing to you in and of itself. As you put your intention and desire in the search, you will be guided to what stirs your heart and lifts your spirit.

Please do not allow the music to become a crutch in your prayer time so that you feel you cannot pray without music. Make your specially chosen music a part of your regular experience. Use it during times of prayer as well as background music during your day. Change your musical selections from time to time. The idea is to spend time prayerfully listening to music and allow it to support your inward journey into times of stillness, silence, and meditation.

If you work in an environment that will allow it, play carefully chosen background music while you work. Many studies have been done on the effects of music on our mood and motivation, so be selective and you'll see positive results.

## *Prayer Practice*

If you are already one who uses music to complement your prayer time, great. Remember to vary your musical selections from time to time. This assures that you will not get locked into any one piece of music. In this way, you are continually open to new opportunities that other musical selections may bring to you.

If you are new to using music as part of your prayer practice, it can be great fun shopping for music that you will enjoy. Ask friends, ask others in your spiritual community if they have recommendations, and then just listen to lots of music that uplifts and inspires until you find the music that stirs your soul. When you hear it, you'll know it - you'll feel it.

Play the music softly in the background as you have your personal prayer time or just let yourself be still and listen, allowing the notes of the music to carry you off to wonderful places of joy, peace, relaxation, and love.

One meditation practice you can use is to listen for a particular note in the musical piece and let it carry you off on a meditative journey. Fall into its rhythm and form, letting it carry you through the song. This can be very revealing as well as stimulating to your creativity.

Let the music begin!

*No negative thinking when lighting your incense; in fact, intentionally set your mind on Godly ideas.*

# 19
## The Use of Incense

*Prayer Anchor:* "*I call upon you, O Lord, come quickly to me; give ear to my voice when I call to you. Let my prayer be counted as incense before you, and the lifting up of my hands as an evening sacrifice" (Psalm 141:1, 2).*

In ancient times, incense was used in religious rituals and ceremonies as a symbolic offering of prayer to God. Incense was also burned each morning and evening as a symbolic demonstration of continued devotion to God.

When incense is burned, the white smoke that travels upward is symbolic of a phrase you may have heard: "sending up prayers to God." The white smoke and the fragrant smell joined together in times past had the connotation of doing that which would call God's attention to our prayers.

In Luke 1:10 we read of an incense offering inside the temple: "Now at the time of the incense offering, the whole assembly of the people was praying outside." When the people outside saw the smoke from the incense, they were to pray. Their prayers would have the added power to travel upward or heavenward to reach God.

In the prayer anchor above, David makes his prayer and asks for a quick response. He states that he wanted his prayer to have the kind of attention as if he were burning incense in God's presence.

When we burn incense as part of our spiritual practice, we can't help but notice the fragrant smell. In addition to the smoke generated by the burning of incense, the smell affects our emotional state. Our emotional state in prayer can either be detrimental if it brings up negative emotions or beneficial to help bring about a more receptive frame of mind as we pray.

When selecting incense you will want to be attracted to the smell. You will want to find it pleasing in order to get the full effect of burning incense during your time of prayer. Do not underestimate the power of your sense of smell. Certain fragrances have the ability to arouse various emotions in us. In selecting incense, you want to attract a fragrance that arouses uplifting emotions for you.

In ancient times, only the priest could light incense in the Temple. It was considered a sacred act and a holy ritual as it symbolized approaching God with a prayer. For this reason I suggest that you keep the act of incense lighting as a sacred act. Wash your hands before handling the incense. It is a symbolic act on your part that you are not holding onto any negativity or error thoughts as you set your conscious intention toward God in prayer. When you light your incense, keep your thoughts toward God, life, beauty, love, wisdom, etc. **No negative thinking when lighting your incense: in fact, intentionally set your mind on Godly ideas.**

Do a little reading up on the various fragrances available in incense form. Incense carries different uses according to their affect on our sense of smell and the energy that it holds. Many of the fragrances for incense are also used in oil form. Some of my personal favorites are frankincense, frankincense combined with myrrh, lavender, sandalwood, orange, orange blossom and sage. You can go strictly by the smell or you can go a little deeper by studying the various mystical properties within the various influences attributed to certain kinds of incense. Experiment until you find what works for you.

## *Prayer Practice*

Wash your hands (and face if possible); set your mental intention by clearing your mind of any negativity and approach the lighting of the incense as a sacred act for the holy purpose of prayer. Put your mind on some divine idea as you light your incense (such as Love, Peace, Harmony, Joy, Beauty, Faith, etc).

When you light the incense, be sure to have an adequate incense holder to catch the ashes as it burns. Then begin your time of prayer. Enjoy the fragrance from the incense. Imagine that the incense gives

136

your prayers power because of how you are affected by your sense of smell and your intentions for answered prayer. You may even want to pray David's prayer: *"I call upon you, O Lord, come quickly to me; give ear to my voice when I call to you. Let my prayer be counted as incense before you, and the lifting up of my hands as an evening sacrifice."*

When your prayer is complete and the incense is burned, clean up the ashes and discard. With these actions you affirm: *"It is done!"* As you toss the ashes away say aloud, *"Amen!"*

The Greeks
identified the
sapphire with Apollo;
it was worn when
consulting oracles.

# 20
# Using Precious Stones

*Prayer Anchor:* *"He made the breastpiece...They set in it four rows of stones. A row of carnelian, chrysolite, and emerald was the first row; and the second row, a turquoise, a sapphire, and a moonstone; and the third row, a jacinth, an agate, and an amethyst; and the fourth row, a beryl, an onyx, and a jasper they were enclosed in settings of gold filigree" (Exodus 39:8-13).*

In the Bible, precious stones are mentioned in numerous places for various purposes. The Queen of Sheba brought precious stones as a gift to Solomon that he might share his wisdom with her; a head piece made of precious stone was placed on David's head after one of his conquests; King David made a generous donation to the temple which his son Solomon was to build, and that donation included many precious stones. When Solomon had the temple built, he had it adorned with precious stones.

In the book of Exodus and the book of Revelation, we see the names of 12 precious stones revealed. In the case of Revelation, the stones were used as a foundation around the Temple of Jerusalem. In Exodus, the stones are used to adorn the breast piece worn by the priest. The number 12 is significant as it stands for wholeness and perfection. The two references have 10 of the 12 stones in common.

In ancient times, precious stones were believed to have mystical powers. In some instances, they were believed to ward off evil and negativity, and to provide protection from enemies. Precious stones also have the implication of great wealth, especially since many of the precious stones spoken of in the scriptures were rare and valuable then as many of them are today.

Whether or not precious stones carry a mystical energy could be debated; a case could be made either way. However, we do know that our ancestors believed that they did indeed have energies that would protect, heal, bring favorable conditions and good fortune. What we also know is that believing has great power. What we firmly believe, we draw to us in related experience.

I enjoy the beauty of precious stones. Some of them can be attained at reasonable prices and are not difficult to acquire. I am one of those people who is open to the possibility that stones from the earth might indeed have an energy that they carry. That energy can be activated with mental belief in that energy to support an idea held in mind.

I do not however suggest that we give away our powerful abilities to draw into our lives that which we desire by relying on a stone to deliver it to us. In the 28th chapter of Job, Job speaks of many precious stones as having great value, but makes the point that they are not the source of God's wisdom.

I do suggest that if one is interested in precious stones to be used in spiritual work, ceremonies, or simply to wear for their beauty, that a study be made of the type of stone to be used for the purpose one desires.

There are many books that list the energy that is attributed to various stones. For example, the sapphire mentioned as one of the 12 stones on the priest's breast piece in the book of Exodus and used to adorn the Temple in the coming age referred to in the book of Revelation, is said to have the energy of wisdom, peace, love, power, and healing. **The Greeks identified the sapphire with Apollo; it was worn when consulting oracles.**

If you desire to draw on the energy of precious stones in your time of prayer, here are my suggestions. After you have done your own study of the type of stone you want to use, do a thorough cleansing of the stone to reset its energy and to release any negative energy picked up from others who may have handled the stone previously. Do this by soaking the stone in sea salt[2] for at least 24 hours; 3 days is better and 7 days is even better.

---

[2] Sea salt may be purchased at Health food stores if it is not available at your regular grocery store.

Take your time studying the energies of the stones. Do your own homework, set your own intentions, and follow your own inner guidance when it comes to using stones. You are your own best guide for what is right and best for you.

## *Prayer Practice*

During your time of prayer or meditation, clasp your stone in your hands and consciously set your mind on what you desire. Whatever stone you choose to use should be in alignment with your prayerful desire. For example, you might use the sapphire if your prayer is related to the energy of wisdom, peace, love, power, and healing.

As you hold your stone, only think positive thoughts about your prayer desire. You may work with your stone on a daily basis if you have a particular prayer request. Set a time length for consistent use of the stone like: 3, 9, 12, or 40 days. After that, take a break, cleanse the stone, and begin use again when you're ready to do so.

Some of the suggestions for stones to use have been mentioned in the scriptures quoted above. Some of my personal favorites are emerald, amethyst, carnelian, beryl, chrysolite (which you'll find as peridot), and sapphire. While I like sapphires I find them more expensive than I prefer to pay for a meditation stone. Some of my other personal favorites not listed in the above scripture are, rose quartz, lapis lazuli, chrysoprase, chrysocolla, tiger's eye, topaz, amber and jade. Check them out and enjoy!

I can't say it enough, so here goes again: Your power is not in the stone. Using the stone may help you focus your mind on your desire, and once you get your desire clearly in mind, you'll bring it into manifestation by the power of God at work in and through you.

There have been times
I have been so busy
with daily routines,
schedules, and to do
lists that I missed
God's answer to
my prayer.

# 21
# *Keep a Journal*

*Prayer Anchor:* *"For whatever was written in former days was written for our instruction, so that by steadfastness and by the encouragement of the scriptures we might have hope" (Romans 15:4).*

I have kept a personal journal seriously for the last 20 years, and sporadically since I was a child. In addition to the therapeutic benefits of writing out my thoughts and feelings, I find great comfort having a written record of major events and the "not so major events" that I have experienced.

As part of my spiritual practice, journaling is a way of life. I keep two journals going at once, my gratitude journal, which I write in a few times each week, and my Master Mind Journal[3] which I write in daily. I write my hopes, goals, dreams, and prayers and sometimes even my complaints in my daily journal. This is more structured and guides me by prompting me to write my goals for the year, month, week, and day. There is a place to write what I'm grateful for on a daily basis and lots of other fun things to do in my journal.

I have given myself permission to be who I am in my journal. I write what my thoughts are at the time, and I write affirmations, denials, and prayers, scriptures to help me work with whatever I am feeling and thinking. It has been a blessing for me to have a private place I can go and share whatever is on my mind and heart without fear of judgment or criticism. I don't make it a practice of criticizing myself in my journal. I accept me as I am with all aspects of my personality and yet I use my journal to encourage me to grow, keep focused on my desire to be the best me I can, and to infuse spiritual inspiration into my day.

---

[3] The Master Mind Journal was designed by Jack Boland, the founder of Renaissance Unity (previously known as Church of Today located in Warren, Michigan). Contact Renaissance Unity to inquire about the Master Mind Journal. Many Unity Churches also sell the Journal as well.

147

As a spiritual tool, I love having what I call a written journey of my faith in God. I can read back over my entries and see how my faith has deepened over the years whereas while in the midst of daily living, I did not recognize my spiritual growth. **There have been times I have been so busy with daily routines, schedules, and to do lists that I missed God's answers to my prayers.** It was not until I looked back over my journal that I was able to see clearly, and in my own handwriting, God's answer to my prayers.

I have my journals from the last 20 years, and occasionally I will go back and see where I was in consciousness as a means of seeing just how far I have come. I remember looking back to one of my earlier journals where I found an entry that read "Dear God, I think I'm going to die." As I read on, a problem was described in great detail and obviously it was from a place of great pain. I continued to read through the journal and four months ahead I would find an entry of praise and celebration. The problem that had devastated me so deeply four months earlier had become a cause for gratitude, appreciation and joy.

I like remembering that story for myself. It reminds me that even if it seems like there is no answer and no hope, if I hang on, keep praying, stay steadfast in my prayer practices, the situation will not only pass, but there will again be cause for celebration. This is the greatest value I find in keeping a journal as a regular spiritual practice. I suspect as long as I am able to write, I will have one.

I keep my gratitude journal tucked away inside my Master Mind Journal. In my gratitude journal I'll write at least 10 things in this journal for which I am grateful. Sometimes I'll write a gratitude letter to God, sometimes I write a gratitude letter to myself, thanking me for all that I do to make my life that which God has guided me to be and do. Sometimes I write gratitude letters addressed to other people, not to send but as a way of just being grateful for that person in my life. My gratitude journal entries are also a joy to review to get a special lift. I get to see how my level of gratitude has grown and be reminded how blessed I really am.

148

Journaling can also be fun for those of us who do it regularly. I sometimes decorate my journals. I enjoy using different colored pens and types of writing instruments. I may even draw a picture or tape a picture in my journal or put a prayer card that really speaks to me in my journal. I let my journal be an active part of my spiritual practice.

One of the reasons I hear people express for why they don't keep a personal journal is that of privacy. In order to really let yourself be totally (and sometimes brutally honest) you must be comfortable that no one will read your entries but you. Do what you must to keep your journal private. This way you can feel free to write your true feelings and thoughts in it. This kind of self-honesty is what enhances the benefits of journaling. "Thus says the Lord, the God of Israel: write in a book all the words that I have spoken to you" (Jeremiah 30:2).

I highly recommend adding journaling to your spiritual practice if you are not already doing so.

## *Prayer Practice*

Get a journal or notebook for your private use. Write in it whatever you want, whenever you want. As a prayer practice, write out your prayers in your journal. Date each entry in your journal; this will help when you look back over what you've done. If you are working on a specific prayer request, write that prayer out completely using positive statements. Write the prayer 9, 15, 21, or 40 times each day until you feel a sense that the prayer has been recorded in your subconscious level of mind. Repetition helps to get the thoughts and prayers into our consciousness, and that is the point where we draw the experience for which we are praying into manifestation.

You may want to keep journals for specific topics or subjects such as a gratitude journal, where you only write about what you are grateful for. You could choose to keep a prayer journal for specifically writing out your prayer desires. There could be a goals journal where you list and write about the goals you plan to achieve and how you will achieve them and your progress reports on those goals. And then, you may keep a journal specifically for your prayer vigils where anytime you conduct a prayer vigil, you would record your desires and subsequent outcomes. There are as many possibilities for journals and journaling as you can think of. The important thing to remember is that your journal can be an important tool for your spiritual journey. Try it, and discover your own appreciation for its benefits.

Have you ever heard it said: "God helps those who help themselves?"

# 22
# Hold a Prayer Vigil

*Prayer Anchor:* "*Four days ago, about this hour, I was keeping the ninth hour of prayer in my house; and behold, a man stood before me in bright apparel saying, 'Cornelius, your prayer has been heard and your alms have been remembered before God'" (Acts 10:30-31 RSV).*

Cornelius was "keeping the ninth hour of prayer." This tells us he was in a 9-hour prayer vigil. In the ninth hour he received a response to his prayer. A prayer vigil is a commitment to pray for a certain length of time - hours, days, or even months. The vigil is usually kept regarding a specific matter.

A prayer vigil is another way to persist in praying for what we desire to manifest. This entire book is about many things we can do to spend more time in conscious communion with the God presence within. The idea of a vigil is to keep our thoughts centered on that which we desire for an extended time period. The more we are focused toward our desire, the closer we are to manifesting our good. We pray with persistence and build our consciousness to the level where, we draw to us that which we are praying to demonstrate.

The secret to successful prayer is to do it. The secret to really successful prayer is to do it more. In the book of Acts, we discover that Cornelius already had a good prayer life. We are told in a previous scripture that he "prayed constantly." This 9-hour prayer vigil was probably normal for him, that is to say, it was a regular part of his spiritual practice. And for him we saw immediate results. The more we build a consciousness of prayer, the more we can expect to get expedient results.

A prayer vigil is usually done when we have some matter before us that causes us to believe it will take a little more prayer energy than our normal prayer practice. We may be aware that a deeper consciousness change in us is necessary and therefore more time in prayer is required. These are the kind of challenges we take to a prayer vigil. Perhaps we have experienced obstacles or concerns that are clearly beyond our own personal actions. A heart and mind focused toward our trust and faith in God to handle the situation will bring the answers we seek.

Many people overlook a prayer vigil as a possible solution to their prayer desires. First of all, a prayer vigil requires a commitment to our desire, and a commitment of our time. When we pray, most of us want God to simply give us what we want, and do it immediately. Cornelius received what seemed like an immediate answer to his prayer. But do not forget this was after 9-hours of prayer not to mention a prayer consciousness he had developed over time from "praying constantly."

The act of a prayer vigil suggests our own willingness to contribute to the solution. In a prayer vigil we invest our time, energy, and mind power to receive the rich dividends of God's promises. **Have you ever heard it said: "God helps those who help themselves?"** When we spend more time in conscious, mind-focused prayer, we are in fact "helping God" to help us.

If we are not willing to put in the time to condition our mind so that we discover, embrace, and accept God's answer to our prayer, the question we should ask ourselves is: "Do I really want God's answer?" We should become still and interrogate ourselves on this question, "Am I really committed to doing what it takes to have God reveal the answer to my prayer?"

A prayer vigil will take us deeper within ourselves to discover God's answer, which may be different from the answer we have in mind. This too may be part of our hesitancy in performing a prayer vigil. If in a one-time prayer, we simply tell God what we want, then we can move on to other things. If we repeatedly pray our prayer with the sincerity of consistency, we may well discover God's will for us is a bit different from what we had in mind. And, yes, sometimes that is not what we consciously want.

Some years ago I did a prayer vigil asking God's guidance on my career. I had a business that was getting by but was not prospering to the level that I desired. I thought that with a prayer vigil, God would make a way for some new business to come my way or perhaps give me some marketing strategies I could use. I prayed the same prayers 3 times a day for 7 days. On the morning of the 8$^{th}$ day I received an answer that was so unexpected that it left me taken aback. I received an answer that meant I was to close my business completely and move to Kansas City, Missouri.

The answer was so far from what I was consciously thinking that I knew it had to be God's answer for me. And yet, I immediately began thinking of the excuses for why I could not do this "far out" thing. Excuses like: I had a four year old son, I'd be a single parent without the extended family support that I was accustomed to, I had a business that was at least paying the bills, if I gave my business a little more I was sure it would grow, I didn't know anyone personally in Kansas City, I'd be moving away from all my friends, etc. The list was long. I let the excuses go on for about two hours. I finally realized that I could not dismiss what I had been given. It was God's answer to the prayer I had initiated and, as crazy as it sounded at the time, I had to do as I was clearly guided.

Four months later I moved to Kansas City. The decision changed my life beyond what I could have ever dreamed. And I have never regretted listening to that still, small voice that revealed itself clearly in me on June 22, 1989: "Move to Kansas City."

A prayer vigil is a good self-test we can give ourselves to discover our level of desire for God's answer to our prayer. If we don't really have a firm desire for the divine right answer to our prayer, it makes no difference whether we receive it or not. Quite frankly, we won't have the consciousness to do right by what we receive or the consciousness to hold on to it.

If I had come to the decision to move to Kansas City by any other means than through my sincere, consistent prayer, I don't know that I would have had the inner strength to follow it through. From a human standpoint, the list of obstacles was insurmountable. Of my personal self, I would have given up after the first few "Are you crazy?" remarks I got from my friends and family. But as I began taking the steps to make the move, the obstacles fell aside in domino fashion. Channels opened up that I did not even know existed. Because I was prayed up, I was of a consciousness that the answer would be revealed to me and I could receive it. My choice to make the move was God-given, and therefore the path of its manifestation was God-driven. In my prayer vigil one of the scriptures I had used was the Lord's Prayer. "Thy will be done."

If your prayer desire is immediate, you may want to stick to a 9-hour vigil or hours in increments of 9. Let the time and the intensity of your prayer desire help decide on the length. You could just as well hold an 18 or 27-hour prayer vigil. An example of the kind of situation that would fit an hourly vigil would be if a loved one was in an emergency surgery situation. You would want to begin your vigil before the actual surgery and go through at least the beginning stages of recovery.

Otherwise, a 9-hour measure of time is generally sufficient, for it can be very powerful. Keep in mind that the length of the vigil makes God no more attentive to your prayer than if you prayed it once and stopped. Your prayer is not to change God or to win favor with God. Your consistent time in prayer will make you and those for whom you pray more receptive to the answer. For this reason, if you are praying a vigil for someone else, if it is possible, have them join in the prayer with you.

If time is not of the essence, you may choose to spread your prayer vigil out over a number of days. I have used vigils of 3, 7, 9, 21 (the number 7 multiplied by 3) and 40 days with success. I suggest these numbers because the ancients believed them to have sacred meaning; you will see them used frequently throughout the scriptures.

If you do decide to conduct a prayer vigil, know that what we call divine intervention reveals itself to a consciousness that is prayed up to receive it. The inflow of Spirit in action is always in motion toward our highest good and is always at work on our behalf.

# *Prayer Practice*

## How to Start

A. Spend the time you need to get clear on your desire.
B. Write out your prayer desire so that you will affirm the same desire each time you pray during your vigil.
C. Decide if the length of your prayer vigil will be over several hours or several days. Decide and commit to it.
D. Select a scripture that you feel speaks to your prayer desire. Some scriptures are powerful and can help you to go deep within to do the prayer work that is needed for your desire. My general recommendations would be the prayer anchors for the chapters in this book.

## Set a Time

If you are doing a 9-hour vigil, you will pray at the same time once every hour for 9 consecutive hours. Set your time when the minute hand would be on the up swing. The idea is that as the minute hand goes up preparing for the next hour, so is your consciousness rising to a new level of receptivity, preparing you for answered prayer. For example, if you start your time to pray at 5:30, you will pray again at 6:30, then 7:30 etc.

If you are praying over several days, decide on the hour or hours you will pray. Be consistent with the time throughout your vigil. Let's say you decide to do a 7-day prayer vigil. Here are some examples to consider in structuring your vigil.

- You could pray at 6:30 a.m. every day for 7 days.
- You could select a specific time to pray in the morning and then again have a specific time in the evening, like 6:30 a.m. and 8:30 p.m. for each of the 7 days.
- You could pray 3 times a day for the 7 days, something like: 6:30 a.m., 12:30 p.m., and 9:30 p.m.
- You could elect to pray your prayer several times in one sitting over each of the 7 days. In this case you would affirm your prayer desire (step 4 below) 3 times or however many times you decide. But decide on the number in advance and be consistent throughout your vigil.

157

Let your intuition be your guide, with these choices.

**What to pray**
1. Begin your prayer time with a time of silence. Just a minute or two will be sufficient.
You are turning your attention away from the outer to within.

2. Read the Lord's Prayer aloud from your Bible, (read from the Bible, even if you have memorized it).[4]

3. Next, read aloud the scripture you selected.

4. Using a phrase of scripture or an affirmation that draws you inward, (the scriptural
phrase does not have to be from The Lord's Prayer or the scripture you selected),
clearly state the prayer desire you have written, with your attention focused within.
Here are some examples of how that might sound:
- *"Christ in me is my hope of glory, I see myself healthy and whole."*
- *"The Kingdom of God is within me, I am guided to my right and perfect employment."*
- *"The Lord is my shepherd I shall not want. All my needs are abundantly met."*
- *"Thy kingdom come, Thy will be done. Divine right answers are revealed to me regarding my relationship with _____."*

If you are praying for someone else, use the scripture directed toward the person using their name. Example:
- *"_____(person's name), Christ in you is your hope of glory, you are healthy and whole."*

---

[4]Whenever possible, and when you are working with a scripture, read it from your Bible. There is a subliminal message about your sincerity and the humility you assume when you hold a Bible in your hand from which to pray, read, or study.

These are examples. Carefully choose what speaks to you and design the prayer that suits you.

5. Make a statement of thanks that reveals your trust in God, and your gratitude for whatever is the divine outcome. I pattern this after the scripture in 1 Thessalonians 5:16-18 which reads: "Rejoice always, pray without ceasing, give thanks in all circumstances; for this is the will of God in Christ Jesus for you."
    Example:
    - "*I celebrate the divine right answer to my prayer. As I continue to hold my prayer desire in my heart, I give thanks, knowing God's will is done.*"

6. End your vigil by saying: "*Father, into thy hands I commend my spirit. I leave my prayer desire and the answer in your hands.*"

Release the prayer and any concern for the outcome. Pay attention to what happens in the coming days. Surely you will notice something has happened. But remember that you have placed the situation in God's hands – leave it there. Let divine order in the situation unfold. If you get anxious, affirm to yourself: "*I trust God to reveal the divine right outcome to my prayer*" – and then do it.

# Part Four

# Prayer Practices To help clear away obstacles

*While you are asleep, your subconscious mind will be working
on the prayer desire you have given it.*

## 23
## Healing Waters

**Prayer Anchor:** *"Go, wash in the Jordan seven times, and your flesh shall be restored and you shall be clean" (2 Kings 5:10).*

In the scriptures and many sacred writings, water has long been used as a healing method. Holy men and women have used water in the spiritual cleansings, healing ceremonies and religious rituals they have performed throughout the ages. Today, many still believe that God's power is active as a healing agent in what is called holy water, water that is used to heal and bless others.

Humankind has always had a close relationship with water. We have always known instinctively it is important to our survival. The earth is made up of nearly 80 percent water. Our bodies are made up of about 70 percent water. We've been told in one form or another that we should drink six to eight glasses of water per day to stay healthy (although today, we're being told other liquids count toward this requirement). And we all certainly know the importance of water to bodily cleanliness. We cannot deny that water and its value have great meaning to our overall well-being.

In our prayer anchor, Elisha tells Naaman to wash in the Jordan River 7 times as a cure to his leprosy. Although with reluctance, Naaman does indeed do as instructed by Elisha, and his leprosy disappears. Naaman's skin is not only healed, but the scripture says that "his flesh was restored like the flesh of a young boy, and he was clean" (2 Kings 5:14).

In the 9th Chapter of the Gospel of John, Jesus heals a man who was born blind. He made mud and spread it on the man's eyes and then told him to "go wash in the pool of Siloam" (John 9:7). The man did as Jesus instructed him; he washed in the pool, and his sight was restored.

Let us not overlook that Jesus insisted on being baptized by John the Baptist, who used the water baptism on all those who came to him. "I baptize you with water for repentance..." (Mt. 3:11) The word "repent" means "to change one's mind." When we pray we are affirming a desire to "change our mind" from whatever we are experiencing in order to embrace whatever we desire to experience. Every prayer we pray involves our need for a change of mind.

One of the ways we may assist such a change is through spiritual cleansing. In this process we "repent" or rid ourselves of any negative or error beliefs and that's where water or the idea symbolized by the use of water comes in. Water represents cleansing. Whether we are immersed in it such as in a baptism, or whether we wash in a pool of it or have some sprinkled over us, we still must change our minds.

Water, in and of itself cannot do the work of changing the mind. However using water can support the inner mental and emotional cleansing as it takes place within. While Jesus asked John for the water baptism for Himself, Jesus is never reported as having used water to baptize. We see that he did recommend water to assist with healings as with the man he told to go and wash in the pool.

Most of us will admit that after a long stressful day at work, a warm bubble bath can help us to relax. Listening to the crashing waves of water from the ocean can help calm an anxious mind. And none of us would dispute how a cool drink of water on a hot summer day can quench our thirst in a way that no other liquid can. Let's face it, there is something about water that we need, enjoy, and appreciate. When it comes to our health and well-being, the value we gain from water must not be overlooked in our overall plan for physical, emotional, mental, and spiritual development.

A spiritual bath for the purpose of mental and emotional cleansing can help prepare us to receive prayerful thoughts and words so that healings can take place on all levels of being. Combined with prayer, what might otherwise be a relaxing time in the bathtub becomes a process of clearing out mental blockages that have previously delayed attracting the good that we desire. The healing qualities of water

166

engaged with the body aid in calming the inner spirit. A calm, relaxed spirit is open, receptive, and ready to accept the words of an earnest prayer.

## *Prayer Practice*

1. Get clear on your specific prayer request. Write it on a piece of paper. Find a sacred scripture or reading that is related to your desire. Whatever you select as your reading, it should be inspiring to you and related to your prayer request.

2. Shower before taking your spiritual bath. A spiritual bath is not for the purpose of cleaning the physical body but a practice in which we come already physically relieved of the grime and dirt collected on the body during the normal course of the day.

Caution: Do not use the same water for your spiritual bath that you used to clean your physical body.

3. Clean the tub after your shower.

4. Prepare your bath water. If you have a particular ingredient(s) that you like to use for spiritual bathing purposes feel free to use it. This is not your perfumed soap or shower gel. Many Health or New Age specialty stores sell packaged bath crystals, herbs, and bath products that are nourishing to the body and may be used to address specific prayers. Customize your bath to make it suitable for you.

Here are a few of my favorites:
>  A. Add 2 cups of Hyssop tea to warm running bath water. Hyssop is mentioned in the Bible for cleansing and healing.
>  B. Combine and mix well the following in a bowl: 2 cups of distilled water, 1 cup of baking soda, ½ cup of Epsom salt, 1 tablespoon of sea salt, 3 drops of lavender essential oil. Mix well, then, pour this mixture in the tub under the warm running water. (Test these ingredients on your skin before using them for a bath).

C. Slice cucumbers in a glass bowl and pour 3 cups of distilled water over the cucumbers. Let this sit for 6 hours as the water takes on the nourishment from the cucumbers. Remove the cucumbers and pour the cucumber water under warm running water for your bath.

5. Now that your bath is ready, stand in front of the tub and recite aloud your scripture or sacred reading 3 times.

6. Get into the tub. Let the water soothe you, support your healing and lift your spirit. Remember to put your reading and your written prayer request close by so that you may reach it without getting out of the tub.

7. Begin applying the water to your body. You may use a container to scoop and then pour water on yourself, scoop the water with your hands, or apply with a clean cloth (preferably one that has never been used before or only used for your spiritual bathing). You will gently apply the water to all areas of your body, not scrubbing but gently applying the water.

Next, recall your reading and begin to concentrate your thoughts on it. You may rest from applying the water to your body to re-read your reading and just relax in the water for a time. The main thing is to keep your mind occupied with your reading as a means of clearing your mind completely before you make your prayer request. If you can totally immerse yourself in the water, do so 7 times. If a complete immersion of your head is not desirable, immerse the face. After about 5 - 10 minutes, your bath should be complete.

8. Just before leaving the tub, read your prayer request aloud three times. Then exit the tub. Pat yourself dry and get dressed. Do not think about your prayer request for 24 hours. If you need to think about something, think about your reading.

This bath is best just before going to bed at night because you will feel very relaxed in mind and body. **While you are asleep, your subconscious mind will be working on the prayer desire you have given it.**

Place your written prayer request somewhere close so that after 24 hours you may see it and read it daily until you are satisfied that something has changed in you as a result of your prayer.

*Whatever the issues are in your life, your heart can lead the way to solving, clarifying, prospering, or healing any situation.*

# 24
# *Dear God Letters*

*Prayer Anchor:* *"Now write what you have seen, what is, and what is to take place after this" (Revelation 1:19).*

Our prayer anchor tells us to write. Write about our experiences, write about the way things are and write about what we desire to take place. Great healings can occur from our being open and honest with ourselves, and the God of our being. When we are not honest with others, we block the potential for intimacy, closeness, and true friendship; but when we are not honest with ourselves, we miss an opportunity to grow, heal, and prosper.

I'll speak to two kinds of letters here, both letters are addressed, "Dear God." The first type of letter involves simply writing a letter addressed to God and saying whatever is in your heart. This is how we "write what we have seen, and what is." Here you are writing a letter as you would to a very dear friend with whom you could share your most intimate secrets, without fear of being judged, criticized, or shamed by a set of shoulds.

This kind of letter opens us up to reveal those things for which our minds and hearts may have no other outlet. Sure we have close friends and family, but still, some things we may want to keep within God and ourselves. In writing this kind of letter, we give ourselves a real opportunity to express our intimate feelings and thoughts for our own personal assessment. The letter is not written out of weakness. This kind of letter is written to gain the inner strength that comes with expressed self-honesty for individual growth and development.

The second type of letter involves not so much focusing on our experiences or things as we perceive them in the present, but what we desire to manifest for ourselves in the future. In many New Thought churches, this letter is prepared on New Year's Eve as a way of setting an intention for the coming year. As a result of time spent in prayer, we write the letter opening ourselves up to demonstrations of answered prayer. This kind of letter can be written any time we desire to bring clarity to our prayerful desires.

The most important thing in writing either of these kinds of letters is to be prayerful and to write from the heart. **Whatever the issues are in your life, your heart can lead the way to solving, clarifying, prospering, or healing any situation.** Writing is a very effective method for expressing that which is in our hearts. "Keep your heart with all vigilance, for from it flow the springs of life" (Proverbs 4:23).

## *Prayer Practice*

Decide on the purpose of your letter and the type of letter you will write. Then settle into your time of prayer in the way that works for you. Your goal is to move into a consciousness centered on God within. Prepare to use affirmations, a sacred reading, or any of the prayer practices in this book in coordination with your writing.

Ask from within that you be guided in writing what is on your heart and mind. Bless your pen and paper before you begin to write. Sit in silent meditation for a time listening inwardly. Address your letter *Dear God*, and then write, write, and then write some more. Feel free to let the pen flow across the pages. Do not judge or criticize yourself as you write.

Sometimes using an outer symbol can help focus your attention and help you stay centered in love, life, wisdom, peace, etc. I have a red heart that I sometimes like to hold in my hand just as a reminder that I want to be guided by divine love within me.

Set your intention to enjoy the writing experience as a prayer. Relax and let Spirit reveal to you what to write.

When your have written all that you desire to write, read what you have written for clarity and assessment. Make changes and adjustments where you desire. Notice if any revelations are brought to your attention. If so, they may be addressed by this or other prayer practices in this book.

First type of letter: Place the letter in a sealed envelope. Hold it in your hands and state your prayer desire regarding that which you have written. Place the envelope in your Bible on a particular scripture that speaks to you. If you don't have a scripture that you particularly feel guided to, use one of these: The Lord's Prayer, the 23rd Psalm, or 1 Corinthians 13. Set a time period for letting the letter rest on your chosen scripture (3, 7, 9, 12, 21, or 40 days). Mark the date on the envelope. Finally, you'll want to release your prayer into the ethers and send them forth to begin working on your behalf. Burn your envelope. As you watch the fire consume your desires written in your letter, know that your prayer has been answered and all is well. Remember to take safety precautions when you burn your letter.

Second type of letter: Place the letter in a self-addressed envelope with your full home address, in case you decide to send it through the mail. You may hold it for a particular time period (3, 7, 9, 12, 21 or 40 days) on a scripture in your Bible and then mail it to yourself. You may also place the letter in a special place in your home. The idea is to let the consciousness you demonstrated in putting your desires in writing become a living reality. Open the letter at the appointed time and remember to celebrate your demonstrations. The churches that make this process part of their spiritual practice will often hold the letter and return it to you by mail at a specified time.

*When we choose to suffer over that which has happened in the past, our own self-love must be called into question.*

# 25
## A few words on Forgiveness

*Prayer Anchor:* "So when you are offering your gift at the altar, if you remember that your brother or sister has something against you leave your gift there before the altar and go; first be reconciled to your brother or sister, and then come and offer your gift" (Matt. 5:23-24).

This scripture reminds us that our prayers are not as effective when we hold unforgiving thoughts in our minds about ourselves or others. If we truly want our prayers to be felt and experienced, we must pray with a receptive mind and heart, free from unresolved issues that will surely block the flow of our good. This scripture tells us to pray with a loving and pure heart. Once our heart is an open channel, the grace of God can flow freely through it, we are changed, and our prayers are answered.

Forgiveness is one of life's most difficult hurdles and yet a hurdle to overcome if we are to live a life of health, happiness, and prosperity. When Peter asked Jesus "How many times must I forgive?" Jesus responded "seventy times seven" (Matthew 18:22 KJV). It seems to me that we are being prepared to know that forgiveness is something we'll have to do all of our lives. No matter what the cause of any upset we may experience, we would do well to learn the tools of forgiveness and keep them close at hand.

If we truly want to live a God-centered life, a spiritual life, a high quality life, we cannot hang on to old hurts from the past. If we want to move forward in love, peace, harmony and prosperity, we learn to forgive and make forgiveness a habit. "Those who say, 'I love God,' and hate their brothers or sisters, are liars; for those who do not love a brother or sister whom they have seen, cannot love God whom they have not seen" (1 John 4:20).

There are many books written on the subject of forgiveness and how to do it. The most important thing about forgiveness, however, is that we do it. The method is not as important as the fact that we release ourselves from the burden of carrying anger, resentment, fear, and worry around with us wherever we go. **When we choose to suffer over that which has happened in the past, our own self-love must be called into question.** Forgiveness is not just a choice we make for ourselves; it is a necessity if we want to be happy, healthy, and prosperous.

I offer my favorite prayer practice for forgiving because it works. What I have discovered is that the one who truly wants to be free from unforgiving thoughts in mind and heart has already taken a major step toward doing the forgiveness work. I also know that it is important to teach our children the importance of forgiveness at an early age. One of the best ways to teach forgiveness is to model it, teach it by example. Our children will be leagues ahead on their spiritual journey if they see us model forgiveness and compassion.

## *Prayer Practice*

Read Psalm 51:10. Write in your journal or a notebook your understanding of what this scripture means, especially as it pertains to your forgiveness issue. This will get you familiar with the scripture and begin to impress it upon your mind as something that can help you through the work you are about to do.

Make a list of those whom you need to forgive. If you are working with one particular situation, write out your description of the experience in detail. Next, write the verse from Psalm 51:10 across the top of the page. Affirm and pray the scripture aloud and then recite the names of those on the list. Each day, for 9 consecutive days, take a fresh sheet of paper and repeat the process from the beginning.

After 9 days, if you do not feel as though the burden of unforgiveness has been lifted or at least eased, repeat the process. Remember "70 times 7" or as many times as it will take to forgive is what you want to commit to.

If there is hesitancy in you around forgiving any particular person on your list, you will want to examine your level of willingness to be free of the inner pain that comes with holding onto that which caused you pain. Do you have difficulty in general with letting go of the past? If hanging on to what pains you is what you choose for yourself, you may be in need of some inner work involving self-love . Here is an affirmation to help you through the 9-day forgiveness process above. Speak it aloud, write it over and over again in your journal and spend time meditating on it.

*"I love myself enough to let go of that which has caused me pain and suffering. I willingly let go of any and all unforgiving thoughts about _____. I prefer to use my energy for productive new opportunities. I am worthy to be free from unloving thoughts, so I can move forward using my energy to love me and welcome new possibilities that await me. I love myself enough to make the conscious decision to let go of the past and to move forward with poise, ease, and under grace."*

If, after the 9-day process, you are still having difficulty forgiving and moving on, first be patient with yourself and secondly be persistent in your efforts to forgive. Sometimes the hurt we feel may take some deeper work to clear out. Set aside some time to examine your level of willingness to forgive by journaling what your thoughts and feelings are regarding the person about whom you hold unforgiving thoughts. Write out your reasons for holding on to the past. Write until you have exhausted all reasons and excuses for holding on to something that is blocking the flow of good coming into your life. Once you have a feeling of readiness, repeat the prayer practice using Psalm 51:10 as your prayer anchor.

If you need to repeat this process, give yourself a 2 or 3-day break and start fresh with a new 9-day process from the beginning.

Often times, the person we need to forgive is ourselves. If this is the case, perform the above prayer practice using your name. Remember you deserve to be free of pain and suffering so that you get to enjoy life and the good that you desire.

*When we are experiencing a "cash flow" challenge, we need to be clear that money is never the real issue.*

# 26
# Money, Money, Money

*Prayer Anchor:* *"But remember the Lord your God, for it is he who gives you power to get wealth..."*
*(Deuteronomy 8:18).*

Let's face it. For many of us, there may have been a time or two when we experienced a temporary cash flow challenge. And, for some of us, we may find ourselves in this uncomfortable place again at some point. What can we do to prayerfully move through it?

I have often been asked if it is OK to pray for money. My answer is yes. If there is a need, we should indeed pray about it. In fact, if we are vigilant in our prayer life, we pray about everything. We know that, apart from God, we have no financial affairs. If we are attentive to our affairs, we go to God within for all of our joys and celebrations as well as any concerns or sorrows.

However it is important to know that whenever we find ourselves in "need," a larger issue is the cause of the lack we are experiencing. In the spiritual law of supply and demand, God has already taken care of the supply side.

Do you remember in the story of the prodigal son, the older son stayed home feeling as though he did not have his father's blessing, and more importantly his father's love? When the younger son who had squandered his inheritance, returned home, the older son was jealous; he had not claimed his inheritance and erroneously believed he did not have access to it. "Then the father said to him, 'Son you are always with me, and all that is mine is yours'" (Luke 15:31).

If we find ourselves believing we do not have access to our full inheritance of supply and every kind of good, let us remember the words the father said to his son "all that is mine is yours." All the good that God is, is already our rich inheritance. If we are not receiving it, demonstrating it, and enjoying it, then we look at the demand side of the spiritual law of supply and demand. **When we are experiencing a "cash flow" challenge, we need to be clear that money is never the real issue.** Unfortunately, money gets blamed for far more stuff than it is even capable of being responsible for. Whenever there is a money issue, you can rest assured that money is innocent.

So, yes, we can indeed pray to receive money, as long as we understand and accept that when we experience a slow down in our cash flow, it is a symptom of a larger challenge related to the demand side of the law. If we just pray to have the money we need come to us, we are addressing our situation with a temporary fix. Whatever is behind the appearance of a slow down in cash flow must eventually be addressed if we do not want to end up in the same situation thirty days later when the bills come due again.

You may already know what the larger challenge is regarding you and money. If not, you can address the demand side of the law by answering some key questions that will reveal what is at the root of your money issue. This personal inventory will help you to identify where your true prayer work should be directed. Here are a few of the best places to look in your life, if cash flow seems to be a recurring challenge.

- What is your overall attitude regarding money, finance, and prosperity?
- Do you pay your bills on time?
- Are you heavily in debt?
- Are you generous in your giving?
- Do you give to spiritual work?
- Are you harboring any unforgiveness toward self or others?
- Do you manage your financial affairs with integrity, honesty, and wisdom?
- Do you willingly give of your time and talent to help others?
- Do you regularly show your gratitude for the blessings in your life?
- Do you have a personal financial plan with wealth-building goals in place?

The answers to these kinds of questions will get at the heart of the matter regarding your cash flow situation. Start with your answers to identify where you may look to resolve the issues. Your answers will reveal what may be blocking your ability to draw to you the money substance you need to do the things that are yours to do. Remember money is never the issue. God is your source, "and all that is mine is yours," says the spirit of God in you, regarding your life and affairs.

There are many books written on money management. Make a study of this area if you are having difficulty demonstrating the level of money supply you desire. You will do well to make a study of the spiritual laws regarding prosperity as well. From a spiritual perspective, you will need to work on your belief about money, the thoughts you hold in mind about money and the words you speak regarding money or your lack thereof. In your prayer, you want to get inwardly connected with the divine understanding that God is your source; our prayer anchor reminds us "for it is he who gives you the power to get wealth."

## *Prayer Practice*

In our prayer practice regarding money, we begin from the truth about money substance. We let Spirit teach and guide us on what we need to know and do for greater demonstrations in our financial affairs.

Follow this 4-Step prayer format:

1. Begin your prayer by acknowledging God's presence within. Let your thoughts be on God as Spirit, Life, Love, and Wisdom.

2. Next, fill your mind with thoughts of peace and harmony. It may help to silently affirm something like: *"I am at peace. I rest in the peaceful presence of God. I am one with the peaceful presence of the Holy Spirit within."* Use what has worked for you in the past to get to the state in consciousness where you are not worrying or even thinking about money, but have put your mind and heart in a peaceful state acknowledging God's presence.

187

3. Ask within something like:
- *Why am I having a limiting experience with money?*
- *What is it in me that is blocking the flow of money substance in my life?*
- *What must I do to claim the wealth and prosperity that is promised as my divine birthright and true inheritance?*
- *What must I change about me in order to demonstrate greater prosperity in my financial affairs?*

Ask each question, then sit, wait, and listen inwardly. Do not hurry through this process. Stay open to Spirit and allow the answers to come to you either during your prayer time or in the days ahead, but be persistent.

4. Close your prayer with a time of gratitude. Let yourself genuinely feel a sense of gratitude for your awareness of God's presence active in you and in your affairs. Give thanks for the blessings already demonstrated in your life. Say a *"Thank you God"* for all the guidance you have received and will continue to receive regarding your financial affairs.

These are the kinds of inner questions you want to take into your prayer time. Ask and you will receive your answers. Your follow-up to the answers you receive will be your new work. As Spirit reveals to you areas for you to work on, you must take action or you will again find yourself in a place of limitation and lack.

From a practical standpoint, begin to bless what you already have. Here are a few examples:
- As money comes to you from any and every channel, immediately give thanks for it. Make it a habit of saying: *"Thank you God for this money to use and enjoy. I accept it gracefully and use it wisely."*

- When you pay your bills, let your attitude be one of gratitude. Give thanks for those creditors who have put their trust in you to pay the bills you have accumulated. Make it important that you operate in integrity with your creditors. Pay them on time. If you are going to be late, call them, don't wait for them to call you. When you pay each bill say: *"Thank you, God, for the money I freely give for the services (or goods) I have received."*

- Practice giving. As soon as you receive money, give 10% of it to the place where you receive spiritual nourishment. Hold the 10% you will give in your hands and say: *"I freely give as I have freely received. As I give, so do I receive. I know that the more I give, the more I am able to give. Thank you, God!"*

Most New Thought Churches and Centers have classes, workshops, and seminars to help you expand your consciousness in this area and other areas of your life. Your life and affairs can be changed as you make a commitment to change. Remember money, or the lack thereof, is never the real issue.

*Every prayer we pray is an idea with its own unique and natural gestation period within our consciousness.*

# 27
## "A Time to Wait"

_**Prayer Anchor:** "I waited patiently for the Lord; he inclined to me and heard my cry. He drew me up from the desolate pit, out of the miry bog-and set my feet upon a rock, making my steps secure. He put a new song in my mouth, a song of praise to our God. Many will see and fear, and put their trust in the Lord"_
_(Psalm 40:1-3)._

In all things there is a time to wait. For some of us, waiting can be our most difficult challenge when we have a desire for which we are praying. In our prayer time we may feel a strong sense of urgency. We want our prayers answered immediately. However, the urgent feeling often grows into anxiety, and anxiety grows to worry, and worry blocks our receptivity to the answer we've been praying for.

Remember what Jesus had to say about worry? Don't do it! "Therefore I tell you, do not worry about your life..." (Matthew 6:25). Worry can be the mental obstacle that delays our good. When we find ourselves in an impatient state of mind, our focus shifts from what we want, to getting something, thus giving our power to what may well be what we do not need or desire.

When we make decisions and choices from our own impatience, it often proves to be less effective and may even be a decision we may live to regret. Whoever said patience is a virtue really had the right idea. Patience can often be the difference between getting what we desire and getting something that brings difficulties with it.

A waiting prayer is one where we intentionally practice waiting in the silence for an answer to our prayer to be revealed to us. Once the inner answer is experienced, we have the strength, will, patience, and peaceful anticipation to wait for the outer manifestation of the response to our prayer. Then we find it easier to be patient while working toward the outer manifestation, since our guidance has come from the spirit of God active within us.

**Every prayer we pray is an idea with its own unique and natural gestation period within our consciousness.** The length of the gestation period can range from the second we make the request to many years in the future and everything in between. Our part will be to trust that there is a divine timing for everything. Our prayer or the idea within our prayer may need time to develop into a strong enough presence to travel from the invisible realm to the physical realm. If we can think of our prayers as seeds being planted in the universal pool of ideas, we may be more willing to give them time to take root and grow into healthy manifestations of magnificent possibilities.

Our prayers may require that the right people and the right set of circumstances be in place before our prayer is demonstrated. Whenever you pray, be willing to give Spirit the time to bring all the right circumstances into perfect alignment. When the answer to your prayer does manifest, if you've trusted God enough to wait, you can rest assured that your highest good will manifest and all who are connected with it in any way whatsoever will be blessed as well.

## *Prayer Practice*

Begin your time in prayer according to your normal practice, or use any of the prayer practices in this book that you are drawn to. Follow the 3-step prayer process below.

1. Pray the words from Psalm 40:1-3. Say the words, pray them, feel them, affirm them 9 times aloud, pausing after verse 3 of each repetition. Then sit in the silence and practice waiting. When we wait in prayer, we are listening inwardly. After a time that you feel is sufficient, start the prayer at verse 1 again until you have done this process the full 9 times.

2. After the 9th recitation, speak your personal prayer request, affirmation, statement, or intention aloud 3 times. Then "wait" on Spirit in silence. I suggest you give yourself at least 30 minutes to an hour of "waiting" for some movement of spirit in your own

consciousness. You are waiting for inspiration, guidance, divine ideas, or a revelation of Truth from within. Sit in the silence for as long as it takes and for as long as you are willing.

3. Close your time of prayer with a few moments of giving thanks for the divine answer that is being revealed to you. Express your willingness to trust God in the process of waiting.

Stay flexible with the number of days you will use this prayer practice. You may receive an answer the first day or it may take many days. Either way, know that whatever time you wait in silence you are preparing for the good that you desire. Trust that Spirit has a natural order for things to occur, and your part is to wait in the silence, knowing the divine right answer will be revealed.

Be aware that a response may come during your "waiting" time or it may come in the course of the days that follow this process. Stay open to what occurs around you and the thoughts that come to you. Spirit may reveal a response through opportunities that come to you, people you meet, or a set of circumstances made available to you. Stay open, and pay attention.

If you are a journaler, this is a great time to journal about the thoughts that come to you from praying this prayer. It will help you to remain open, and allow whatever work needs to occur in the invisible to be done, without anxious interfering thoughts from you.

While you are in this prayer process of "waiting" on your answer from Spirit active in you, don't talk about your prayer request to anyone unless you are inwardly guided to do so. If you are truly "waiting on the Lord" as our prayer anchor says, your need to talk about this process with someone else may be an indication that you are getting impatient, which is the direct opposite of what this prayer is about. When your response has come, then you may choose to share it with others.

*A spiritual community is the place where we expect to find others who have made it their intention to live a life centered in spiritual ideals.*

# 28
## The Value of a Spiritual Community

*Prayer Anchor:* *"Are any among you sick? They should call for the elders of the church and have them pray over them, anointing them with oil in the name of the Lord. The prayer of faith will save the sick, and the Lord will raise them up and anyone who has committed sins will be forgiven. Therefore confess your sins to one another, and pray for one another so that you may be healed. The prayer of the righteous is powerful and effective" (James 5:14-16).*

I have so often visited hospitals and nursing homes where people had no spiritual community supporting them, praying for them, visiting them or even remembering them with an occasional card. Not because the community forgot about them, but because they did not get involved when they could have.

Too many times I have been asked to conduct the funeral or memorial service of a person unknown to me and not a member of our spiritual community or any other spiritual community. I am certainly happy to assist the family in this situation. However, I have to be coached as to who the person was, the kind of life they lived, and the contributions they made and left as their legacy.

Some years ago a family came to me, saying their mother had made her transition and the family had been to several churches trying to find someone to conduct a funeral service for their mother. They said their mother believed in God but never really attended a church and had no connection with a faith community. One of the three children did have a faith community in which she was involved, but they did not perform services for anyone who was not a member. They wanted their mother to have what they believed to be a proper burial and came to me frustrated at the rejections they had received. Of course I performed the Service. It was small with just a few people attending. No one spoke from the family and few friends who had gathered. I left the small gathering of people at the cemetery that day wondering why a woman had lived to 80 plus years and seemed to not have connected with others to any great extent. Why? At this point, I could only wonder.

Our prayer anchor illustrates that a spiritual community can be of great value to us. We have a place to go where we feel comfortable asking for support and giving support. It is important to establish ourselves and align ourselves with a support system before we need one. In this way we grow to higher levels of our spiritual potential when we engage in life with others through service, giving, receiving, caring, and sharing ourselves with other children of God.

**A spiritual community is the place where we expect to find others who have made it their intention to live a life centered in spiritual ideals.** Spiritual principles guide and direct us to live out the divine ideas of love, faith, wisdom, peace, harmony, joy, and prosperity. The foundation for everything that is done is centered in these divine ideas. Divine love is at the core of the mission, "You shall love the Lord your God with all your heart and with all your soul, and with all your mind...You shall love your neighbor as yourself" (Matthew 22:37-39).

When we are an active part of a spiritual community, we have a place where we are accepted and embraced no matter what our life circumstances. It is a place of support, friendship, fellowship, and celebration. While each member will grow spiritually at his or her own pace, the collective community will grow to the level of making a difference in the world. We have a loving place where we are reminded of God's love within us and encouraged to express that love in the outer on a daily basis.

The greatest benefit however is the commitment we make to our own spiritual growth and our personal revelation of truth. We make a conscious intention to learn and live the teachings of the spiritual community that we have been drawn to. The gift we receive is an expanded spiritual consciousness and the discovery of our true self.

We gain all this for having allowed ourselves to be supported on our journey, and for giving support to others on theirs.

When we find a spiritual community where we feel safe to be who we are as we grow, and where we are receptive to the teachings, we ought to consider being actively involved. Service enhances our overall spiritual growth and provides us with an outlet for our spiritual gifts and talents.

Let the light of God show forth from you through sharing yourself and supporting others in whatever way you are guided. "Let your light shine before others, so that they may see your good works and give glory to your Father in heaven" (Matthew 5:16).

## *Prayer Practice*

Most spiritual communities have some kind of prayer or chaplain ministry where members are ready to pray one-on-one with those who ask. If you do find yourself desiring prayer support, do not hesitate to ask for it. People who have received the calling to pray with and for others love to do it and will give you their best and highest expression of God's love within them. Ask.

Consider getting involved in a ministry that prays for others. Your own prayer life will be greatly enhanced as you pray with and for others. If directly praying with others is not your calling, do find some area where you may volunteer in your chosen spiritual community. I have discovered that those who are involved and active do enjoy a deeper spiritual experience – in their own personal lives and with others in the community.

You don't have to be a formal member of a prayer ministry to pray for the members of your spiritual community. Make this part of your regular prayer practice. Pray for the pastor, minister, spiritual leader, and all who serve in ministerial and leadership roles. The stronger and more prayed up they are, the more they can give to the community as a whole. You want them to know that they are surrounded by others who see them expressing God's life, love, and wisdom in all that they do. With the prayers of others, they will continue to be blessed in their own individual lives. And, when their personal affairs are harmonious, it will directly affect their ability and desire to effectively serve the community as a whole.

Pray for all the members of your faith community that all may live and express the presence and power of God individually and as a collective body. See your spiritual community being an example of peace on earth.

In your time of prayer, visualize your whole community of faith bathed in a white light of God's presence. See the individual members centered in peaceful harmony with each other while serving and living God's will for their lives. Affirm that the entire community demonstrates the purpose attributed to the organization's mission as a whole. "For just as the body is one and has many members, and all the members of the body, though many, are one body, so it is with Christ" (1 Corinthians 12:1).

*Whenever we witness God's compassionate attention to the prayers of others, we are moved by it and desire the same for ourselves.*

# 29
## Praying the Psalms

*Prayer Anchor:* *"Where can I go from your spirit? Or where can I flee from your presence? If I ascend to heaven, you are there; if I make my bed in Sheol, you are there. If I take the wings of the morning and settle at the farthest limits of the sea, even there your hand shall lead me, and your right hand shall hold me fast" (Psalm 139:7-10).*

The Book of Psalms is one of the most popular books in the Bible. The Psalms are a collection of poems, hymns, and various kinds of prayers. The prayer anchor for this chapter gives a good overall theme for the book itself. It reveals the timeless lesson that we all want and need to know: it tells us we can never be separated from God.

Psalm 139 confirms for us that no matter where we go, or what we do, we are never out of the far reaching hand of God. We discover that we can count on God to be there for us even when we are not living up to the best of who and what we are. The message is, wherever we are, God's loving presence is there also. The hand of God is steady. It holds us through the falls we sustain to soften the hurt, lifts us up from the errors we make, guides us through times of change, nurtures and nourishes us as we grow. But no matter what, indeed the hand of God is always upon us.

In the Psalms we find writings that re-confirm over and over God's presence is always with us. We see it expressing as strength, trust, praise, thanksgiving, celebration, and compassion between God and the writers of this inspirational book. We feel a deep connection and empathy with the authors of the various Psalms as we read them. **Whenever we witness God's compassionate attention to the prayers of others, we are moved by it and desire the same for ourselves.** The Psalmist lives in hope, and we get a glimpse of that hope for ourselves as we read through the powerful words of devotion, love, and humility toward God.

Because the Psalms have been prayed and sung for thousands of years their vibratory energy can not help but be one of faith, strength, and power. The one who prays them with the spiritual discernment of an evolving consciousness will demonstrate results beyond measure.

It is important to get into the feeling of the words and not get stuck in the literal wording of some of the Psalms. The writers wrote from their own experience and the consciousness through which they lived at the time. You and I can pray these same Psalms, the same words, and apply an expanded consciousness that is relevant to our spiritual understanding.

For example in some of the Psalms you will read of the anger and desire for vengeance on the part of the one who is praying. Read the words understanding that the writer wants to portray the deep feelings of pain and the level of suffering that only God can heal. If you have ever had moments of deep anger you may remember that your thoughts may not have been very loving in that moment. So be gentle with the Psalmist as his pain was deep for him and he trusted God enough to pour them out in the one place he was sure they could be addressed properly - to God.

For you, as you read the words, know that it takes great strength and trust in God to be completely open and honest about whatever you are feeling. Your goal is to attain that level of openness and honesty in your unfolding relationship with God. In this light, you will pray with the same knowing that the Psalmist did. God can heal any and every error thought, belief, and action we have created in our consciousness. So lay them out for God to heal rather than ignore them and be forever bound to them.

In reading the words, allow the movement of spirit within you to heal, lift, bless, and prosper whatever situation you are growing through. The Psalmist prayed from right where he was in consciousness, and this precipitated the spiritual growth and unfoldment that allowed him

206

to discover "The Lord is my Shepherd. I shall not want" (Psalm 23:1). "For it was you who formed my inward parts; you knit me together in my mother's womb. I praise you, for I am fearfully and wonderfully made." (Psalm 139:13, 14); "The Lord is my light and my salvation; whom shall I fear?" (Psalm 27:1). "Great is the Lord, and greatly to be praised; his greatness is unsearchable" (Psalm 145:3). The testimonies of the Psalmist go on and on.

Here are a few of my favorite Psalms and some of the themes connected with each one.

**Psalm 23** Pray this Psalm when your prayer desire is for: Protection, healing of any kind, to address financial concerns, to cure thoughts of lack and limitation, to reduce feelings of fear or worry, to stimulate inner peace, divine guidance, comfort and gratitude, for the release of a loved one who has made their transition.

**Psalm 91** Pray this Psalm when you desire: To reconfirm God's protection, to control anxious and fearful thoughts when you are facing difficulties.

Verses 14-16 are God's response to the love, loyalty, and trust the Psalmist demonstrates toward God. Specifically pray this part of the prayer when you feel the need to know God's love, protection and blessings are upon your life.

**Psalm 112** Pray this prayer when you desire: To put God first in your life, success and prosperity for a new endeavor, guidance in business affairs, protection in business transactions, to develop a consciousness of charitable giving.

**Psalm 119** This Psalm is the quintessential prayer/meditation for attaining divine guidance. Also pray this Psalm to strengthen your faith and to develop discipline in spiritual matters.

**Psalm 121** Pray this prayer for safety in traveling for yourself or loved ones.

**Psalm 139** This is a great Psalm to pray and meditate upon when you feel: lost, alone, separate from God, fearful, in need of divine guidance, unworthy, low in self esteem, the need for a boost in self-confidence, unloved, the need of assurance that your loved ones are in God's care and keeping.

**Psalm 150** This prayer celebrates God at work in our lives. Pray as a prayer of gratitude and thanksgiving.

## *Prayer Practice*

I suggest first reading through the entire book of Psalms and making a personal list of those that speak to you. Use this list from which to make your selections when you choose to use this particular prayer practice.

Select one of the Psalms that speaks to you and addresses your particular prayer desire. Read through the entire Psalm to understand the theme. Select the verse(s) from the Psalm that particularly speak to your prayer request to be used as your prayer.

See the prayer practice in the chapter entitled: "A few words on Forgiveness" for an example of using one verse from the scripture as a prayer. The scripture used is from Psalm 51. Its theme is forgiveness. David had committed an act for which he sought forgiveness. We used one verse from that Psalm, verse 10, as the prayer for forgiveness. I am suggesting you do the same thing here. Use your own guidance and intuition to select the verse or verses that address your prayer desire.

- Set your intention on the number of days to pray the prayer you have selected (3, 7, 9, 21, 40).
- In your journal prayerfully write the verse or verses you will use in your notebook 3 times each morning, followed by your specific prayer request.
- Each evening just before going to sleep, prayerfully read your selected verse 9 times aloud (from your Bible) meditating on the words and their meaning. Do not revisit your specific prayer request during this part of the process.

- During the length of this prayer practice stay open to ideas and opportunities that are sure to present themselves. Stay open and prepare to take action on any guidance received.

Another method of praying the powerful prayers from the Psalms is to pray on the scripture you select verse by verse. Take one verse per day until you have prayed, meditated and journaled on the entire Psalm. Take one final day to meditate on the entire Psalm. Ask in prayer for the meaning the verses of this Psalm have for your life and its value to your prayer desire. Journaling through this process can be very enlightening and empowering. The key is to pray the Psalm that addresses your own particular purpose for prayer.

For example if you were working on forgiveness you could set aside 20 days for this prayer work (there are 19 verses and 1 day for the entire Psalm). On day 1 you would prayerfully read verse 1 only. After meditating on the verse and asking inwardly for its meaning for you, journal any thoughts revealed to you. Repeat the process until you have completely meditated on the entire Psalm.

Psalm 119 may certainly be prayed verse by verse, because it is the longest of the Psalms. It would take 177 days to complete. If you wanted to make a prayer of this in a shorter time, you could divide it up over a 22-day span, taking 1 section per day. Each section contains 8 verses. It is well worth the prayerful study and meditation as it helps to deepen one's faith and understanding of God's law. It examines how God works in our lives and how we are to work toward fulfilling God's plan.

# Part Five

# Prayer Practices
# For a deeper
# Spiritual Experience

*When we humble ourselves, as we do by fasting and praying, we are doing our inner preparation work which sets the stage for answered prayer.*

# 30
# Fast and Pray

*Prayer Anchor:* *"Go, gather all the Jews to be found in Susa, and hold a fast on my behalf, and neither eat nor drink for three days, night or day. I and my maids will also fast as you do. ...On the third day, Esther put on her royal robes and stood in the inner court of the king's palace.... As soon as the king saw Queen Esther standing in the court, she won his favor and he held out to her the golden scepter that was in his hand....The king said to her, 'What is it, Queen Esther? What is your request? It shall be given you, even to the half of my kingdom'" (Esther 5:1-2).*

The story of Queen Esther has long been one of my favorite stories. It has intrigue, romance, mystery, divine intervention, and a happy ending - many of the qualities we enjoy seeing on a big screen at the movies.

When her people were faced with a threat to their lives, Esther found herself in the position of spiritual leadership, and she rose to the occasion in grand style. We don't know what Esther's prayer life was like before she called a 3-day fast and prayer vigil, but somehow she knew this was the thing to do.

In the canonical Book of Esther, it tells us that Queen Esther asked all the Jews to fast on her behalf and neither eat nor drink for three days, night or day. She said she would be fasting also. After three days she would go and ask the king to spare their lives, knowing she would be putting herself in danger by doing so.

What you may or may not know is that after the Book of Esther had been translated from Hebrew into Greek, six additions totaling 107 verses were added to Esther's story. They are recorded in what is called the Apocrypha. There the story is told a little differently in that Esther does not call a fast but she does hold her own 3-day prayer vigil.

In Chapter 14, of the Apocrypha, Queen Esther changes her clothing from her royal attire and puts on "garments of distress and mourning...she utterly humbled her body, and every part that she loved to adorn she covered with her tangled hair. And she prayed" (Esther 14:2 Apocrypha).

She prayed for three days, and on the third day, when she ended her prayer, "She took off the garments in which she had worshiped, and arrayed herself in splendid attire. Then majestically adorned, after invoking the aid of the all-seeing God" (Esther 15:2 Apocrypha). Esther goes before the king, putting her own life in danger for doing so and the king not only listens to her but also gives her what she asks. The lives of her people are spared and justice is brought about for the culprit who attempted to have the Jews killed in the first place.

What a story. One version speaks to fasting and the other to praying. They are both correct. The ancients accompanied praying with their time of fasting. These two powerful spiritual practices together make for the movement of spirit on our prayers. A fast is a set period of time we take to do cleansing work. We fast by abstaining from negativity and error thinking as mental and spiritual cleansing work; we fast for inner physical cleansing by abstaining from solid food. Combined, fasting for mental, spiritual and physical cleansing forms a ripe consciousness for grand new possibilities.

In ancient times and under religious practice, fasting was thought to be a humbling experience that demonstrated the faith and discipline necessary to prepare for approaching God with specific requests. In the scriptures where there was fasting and praying, God found favor on those who prayed; they felt and believed that their prayers were answered because they humbled themselves by fasting and because they approached God with reverence through focused prayer. "So we fasted and petitioned our God for this, and he listened to our entreaty" (Ezra 8:23). They fasted and prayed because they got results.

As a spiritual practice, fasting has two levels. The first level occurs when we do a mental cleansing. We fast from negative thoughts and feelings. This clears the mind and prepares us mentally to receive the wisdom of Spirit from within. The second level involves fasting from solid food for a physical bodily cleansing. At this level, we gather the support of the physical body to aid a more complete cleansing process. When the bodily functions involved in the whole digestive process are set free to relax, that unused energy is directed to support the mental focus toward purifying our thoughts.

Fasting and praying brings together the physical, mental, and spiritual aspects of our being. In this way, we give our prayer request the full support of all that we are. We set ourselves apart from our normal routines and declare this prayer request a high priority in our lives and therefore the answer becomes a high priority for the power of God within us.

If you choose to incorporate fasting from solid food into your spiritual practice, it is extremely important that you do not do so without the advice of your health care professional. If you have certain ailments and health conditions, fasting from solid food can cause more harm than good. So please get professional help before you fast. I can only share with you my experience with the hope that it helps you develop your own with the assistance of your health provider.

I have fasted for 1, 3, 7, 9 and 21 days on varying occasions for different purposes. What generally works for me these days is 1 or 3 days. When I have done an extended fast it was with very specific mental, physical and spiritual goals, goals that were prayerfully directed.

An extended fast anything over 7 days, I would not do alone, that is without some kind of support system and most likely under medical watch. When I did my 21-day fast, I did so with a group of like-minded friends who were also fasting and praying during the process. We supported each other and served as a watchful eye in assuring that we did the disciplined things one must do during this kind of fast to keep healthy and focused.

When I fast, I ingest all fresh juices and lots of water. These days I use fresh organic vegetables for juicing, and to a very limited extent I'll juice some fruit. I do not believe in all water fasts. I tried it once, and for my level of health, it was too hard on my body.

After about 3 days of fasting and praying, my experience is that my dreams are more vivid and my meditations are deeper. I feel more at peace and do not require as much sleep as usual. Whenever I have incorporated fasting from solid food with my prayers, I have journaled. I keep notes on the experience paying careful attention to the mental, spiritual, and physical changes in me during the process. I have always been blessed with the many benefits I receive from combining fasting with my prayers.

I would suggest you read up on fasting before doing your first fast. There are lots of books written on the subject. Do your personal homework if you are serious about taking fasting to this level. I'm not attempting to give you health care advice, however there are many other healthful suggestions to complement your fasting that you will want to know about. For example most books that speak of fasting will tell you to eat easily digestible foods in the days prior to and after your fast – no dairy, no meat, no animal fat at all. These are the kinds of things you need to know if you want fasting and praying to be a really successful event.

I have discovered that my body enjoys a good fast from solid food from time to time. When I do fast I have increased energy, mental and spiritual clarity. Quite frankly when I fast from solid food and negative thoughts together, I feel great.

If you are not in a situation where you may fast from solid food, or simply choose not to do it, you may fast from negative thinking and this is certainly effective.

**When we humble ourselves, as we do by fasting and praying, we are doing our inner preparation work which sets the stage for answered prayer.** In this way, we condition our mind with faith and great expectancy.

## *Prayer Practice*

Get specific on your prayer desire and the purpose for adding fasting to your prayer.

- Put your prayer in writing.
- Decide on the length of your of your fast (1, 3, 7, 9, 21, or 40). I've never done a prayer/fast longer than 21-days. However in the Gospels it is mentioned that Jesus fasted and prayed for 40 days. I would be extremely careful in deciding on a 40-day fast and would not do it unless under medical guidance.
- Gather the items you will need for your fast. It is important to have what you need at hand for your fast. It will help you to stay focused and disciplined toward your goal.
- Set your fast in motion, and begin your prayer. Pray your prayer at least three times each day of your fast. You'll discover a greater value in your fasting the more time you spend in prayer. So do plan to spend at least 1 full hour in prayer each of the 3 times you pray per day. Your prayers have added power when you give yourself time to sit in the silence with your prayer request.

Remember you are fasting from negative thoughts as well as solid food. You will want to limit watching TV, reading newspapers, and listening to the radio, as these places are where we pick up so much negativity, many times without even realizing it.

When you pray and fast for a specific purpose it is also a good time to bring in some of the other prayer practices talked about in this book: you might light candles, burn incense, take a spiritual bath, etc. Plan to enjoy the experience; you'll gain even greater blessings if you do.

God will give us whatever gifts we ask, if we are indeed sincere about helping, serving, and caring for others.

## 31
## *Know your Spiritual Gifts*

*Prayer Anchor:* "At Gibeon the Lord appeared to Solomon in a dream by night; and God said, 'Ask what I should give you.'... 'Give your servant therefore an understanding mind to govern your people able to discern between good and evil; for who can govern this your great people?' It pleased the Lord that Solomon had asked this. God said to him, 'Because you have asked this, and have not asked for yourself long life or riches, or for the life of your enemies,...I now do according to your word. Indeed I give you a wise and discerning mind; ...I give you also what you have not asked, both riches and honor all your life.'" (1 Kings 3:5, 9-13).*

As a child in Sunday school, I heard people talk of the Wisdom of Solomon. In the church where I grew up, we often talked about Bible characters, but for some reason Solomon was one that intrigued me. I wanted to know how Solomon got to be so wise. What made him so special that God had blessed him with such wisdom that he would be admired and talked about thousands of years after he was long gone?

Not until I was an adult did I read 1 Kings Chapter 3. I learned that Solomon was a praying man who loved God and wanted to serve God with his whole heart. "Solomon loved the Lord, walking in the statutes of his father David" (1 Kings 3:1). He received wisdom from God because he was open to it and he asked for it. That's it. Solomon wanted to live up to the mighty responsibility of being king placed upon him. His desire was so strong that when God came to him in a dream and asked him what he wanted, his response was: Wisdom!

The added bonus in the story is that God heard Solomon's request and was pleased that Solomon had not asked for things or that which would suggest selfish gain. Solomon desired wisdom not for himself, but in order to serve God and the people of Israel. For his humility, God granted to Solomon both riches and honor to be enjoyed for the rest of his life. Solomon is thought to be the wisest man in the Old Testament, but he is also thought to be the wealthiest in the entire Bible.

Wisdom is one of many spiritual gifts identified in the Bible. It is one of many gifts that God has made available to us when we choose to serve God by helping others. We all have spiritual gifts. They show up in our lives as those things that we have a natural interest and talent for; skills that fit well with our purpose in life. Solomon was chosen as heir to the throne succeeding his father. David had been a loved king and under his leadership Israel grew and prospered. Solomon knew he would need wisdom in such an awesome leadership role as being the king of Israel. Wisdom was what he needed to serve God to the highest of his ability and God granted it and so much more.

Whatever we are called to do or for whatever our purpose, our Creator wants us to have what we need to fulfill the task. You can recognize your spiritual gifts by the things that you like to do, and the things that you have a natural talent for. These are the kinds of things people ask you to do for them or help them do. These are the kinds of talents you willingly share to serve God and help others.

"To each is given the manifestation of the Spirit for the common good. To one is given through the Spirit the utterance of wisdom, and to another the utterance of knowledge according to the same Spirit, to another faith by the same Spirit, to another gifts of healing by the one Spirit, to another the working of miracles, to another prophecy, to another the discernment of spirits, to another various kinds of tongues, to another the interpretation of tongues. All these are activated by one and the same Spirit who allots to each one individually just as the Spirit chooses" (1 Corinthians. 12:7-11).

In this scripture we see many spiritual gifts identified. When they are used for the common good or to help others they are spiritual gifts. Others can be found by being open to them as you read through the scriptures.

"We have gifts that differ according to the grace given to us: prophecy, in proportion to faith; ministry, in ministering; the teacher, in teaching; the exhorter, in exhortation, the giver, in generosity; the leader in diligence; the compassionate, in cheerfulness" (Romans 12:6-8).

There are varieties of gifts to be used in service to God and many opportunities to share them. Each person is to use their God given gifts for the nourishment and uplifting of others in unselfish service. **God will give us whatever gifts we ask, if we are indeed sincere about helping, serving, and caring for others.**

Like Solomon we can ask from within to receive the gifts we need to be and do what God has guided us to do. When we say yes to God's plan for our lives, we should ask to be strengthened in those areas that will allow us to serve to our highest ability.

Solomon was blessed with riches and honor for the humility he expressed in his sincere desire to follow the divine path laid out before him to be king of Israel. Solomon knew he could not thrive in the awesome tasks before him from his ego or personality; he needed and wanted the wisdom of God. He demonstrated his true greatness, when he asked God to provide what he needed to follow his divine path. He simply asked, and God answered.

## *Prayer Practice*

This is the prayer practice of an unselfish heart. The purpose is to have Spirit reveal from within the gifts that are especially yours to be used to serve God and to help others.

Write each of these 15 spiritual gifts on an index card, 1 per card: Wisdom, knowledge, faith, healing, working of miracles, prophecy, discernment, speaking in tongues, interpretation of tongues, ministering, teaching, exhortation (encouragement), generosity, leadership, compassion.

- In your time of prayer, read 1 Corinthians 12 in its entirety.
- Take 1 index card per day to meditate on. Hold the card in your hand, and, when you are in a relaxed and prayerful state, focus your attention inwardly and say something to the effect *"God within me, fills my desire to be of service. I am divinely guided now."* Repeat this several times.
- Spend the remainder of your time in prayer, meditating upon the word on the index card. Repeat the word several times. Do not try to force an inner response, you want a natural, spirit guided revelation to the gifts that are yours to be used in service.
- Close your prayer time with a prayer of gratitude for the inner guidance to discover your spiritual gifts.
- Carry the card with you throughout the day. Look at it occasionally during the day as a reminder that you are seeking an inner response to that word from Spirit. Are there any opportunities to express that particular gift during the day? During this time especially, notice any outer messages you may receive from others. Notice the situations you find yourself in, always with an open mind to discover the spiritual gifts you could bring to the experience. Spirit reveals our answers in a variety of ways, so stay open and stay in tune with your desire to discover your spiritual gifts.
- At the end of the day write on the back of the cards any responses and reactions you received regarding the gift you were working with for the day.
- Repeat this entire process, using 1 card per day until all the index cards have been included in your prayer.

Since there are 15 gifts listed, this process will take 15 days to complete. Go through the same process with each word. From some words you may receive a very strong sense that you have this as a gift, from others you may have a lesser reaction. During this process journaling will be very helpful. Write out the experiences that you have and what comes to you during meditations. Take the time to assess what you have received in prayer and what you discerned overall regarding this process. The key is to stay open.

After you have completed the 15-day process, you should be able to narrow your list down to about 3-5 gifts. Take those gifts to 3 or 4 people who are very close to you and who know you well. Ask them if they think you have any of these qualities already. This will narrow your list down to about 2-3 gifts and these are the ones you focus on. Don't miss this step. Oftentimes those close to us can see in us what we cannot see ourselves. When 2 of your 3 people agree on the same gift, you can feel safe to include it as one of your gifts.

In your next available prayer time affirm: *"I am grateful for the spiritual gifts of _____ so that I may be of maximum service to God and those around me. Thank you, God."*

Find a place to serve where you can express the gifts you have identified. If you do this process prayerfully, you will be guided to the spiritual gifts you are to share with others and a place to joyfully express those gifts through service.

By engaging in this prayer practice, you will open yourself up to new opportunities to share your spiritual gifts through service. Allow yourself to be guided to a place to volunteer and begin immediately. And, although service is its own reward, you can expect to receive with the same generosity with which you give, the confirmation of your spiritual gifts and the riches and honor that you so earnestly deserve.

We think we're
calling God, but
chanting is
God calling us.

# 32
# *Chanting*

*Prayer Anchor: "When you are praying, do not heap up empty phrases as the Gentiles do; for they think that they will be heard because of their many words. Do not be like them, for your Father knows what you need before you ask him" (Matthew 6:7-8).*

Chanting has a long history in religious and spiritual practices. Chanting can be described as a word or phrase that is repeated in rhythmic form with or without music. What determines if chanting is a religious or spiritual practice is the words or phrases used, the intention behind it, and the desire to gain what focused repetition can do for the mind, heart, body, and soul.

When picketers march around a building repeating over and over their statements of complaint, this is also chanting. While it is chanting, it does not come under the heading of religious and spiritual practices. When the words or phrases we speak in rhythmic repetition are Godly ideas or ideas related to our spirituality, this is chanting as part of a prayer practice.

Reading the prayer anchor for this chapter, it could be erroneously interpreted that Jesus is against repetition of words when we pray, but Jesus' statement is more concerned with "empty phrases" being repeated under the guise of praying. Empty phrases are words that have no foundation in Truth. They have no feeling and no sincerity behind them. They are not positive or uplifting in quality and character. They are worry statements, begging and pleading toward an unwilling God. These empty phrases are often made as promises of devotion by one who may have no true commitment to keeping his/her word.

Jesus makes the point that our prayers should not be empty words but rather words and phrases of Truth and divine love. The words that we would speak in repetition should be words that uplift, inspire, bless, heal, and prosper. Our repetitions should be toward acknowledging God's presence and power within us.

We don't speak "many words" with the intention to contact God or to get God to hear our prayers. This is not the purpose behind chanting for spiritual purposes. Always our prayers are to change us, not God. Our repetition allows us the opportunity to anchor in our conscious and subconscious levels of mind that God within is always present and available to us. We repeat empowering phrases so that we can align ourselves with the grace and power of God within.

Once we experience the deep communion with God that is possible through chanting, we realize God has heard us from the first word. We've simply activated our desire. We come to know first hand that "God already knows what we need" before we ask him. In the case of chanting, we need to feel God's presence even if we call it something else. We chant to have a conscious experience with God, to be fully aware of our oneness with our Creator and all of creation. This is what chanting for spiritual and religious practice can do for the one who sincerely wants to experience God's presence through prayer.

When we chant, we may think we are calling forth God from within so that God may hear us and listen to our prayer requests. But actually our chanting prepares us to hear the still small voice of God within. **We think we're calling God, but chanting is God calling us**. A simple chant turns into a meeting with God, a divine appointment with our Creator. We may have thought we had an agenda before meeting God in prayer, but we soon discover the experience itself is really a gift and the opportunity to be still and know God.

## *Prayer Practice*

In western religions we don't make chanting a part of our spiritual practice in the same way that our brothers and sisters in the east do. So in the course of your own spiritual community you may not have access to chanting on a regular basis. Even so, there are many recorded tapes and CD's that will help you if chanting is of interest to you. And yes, you can have a deep and profound experience by using a CD or tape as your guide.

It may take some trial and error to get the chant that speaks to you, but it will be worth it if you are serious about adding this to your spiritual practice. The important thing is to be patient with yourself. Learn what the words that you chant mean, and then learn the chants so that you may speak them along with the tape until you no longer need the tape and can do the chants on your own.

You may even want to form a group in your spiritual community who will join together and chant as a prayerful experience. Great value can be gained when each member shares his/her individual experiences.

Also make up your own phrases to chant. Whatever you desire to experience, chant it. Begin saying it over and over again, and a rhythm will emerge. Stay with it and let it unfold for you. Some years ago I wanted to feel God as love in me. I began affirming over and over again "God is love, God loves me." I first said it hundreds of times during the day and finally began to take the words in prayer. As I inhaled, I would say 'God is love', as I exhaled; I would say "God loves me." Focusing on breathing helped to form a pattern that soon took me deeper into myself until I reached a place within where I knew the words that I was saying were true.

Just remember Jesus' warning. Do not heap up empty phrases, but consciously speak with focused repetition words of Truth, wisdom, love, and power, and chanting will be a great blessing to your spiritual growth.

*As part of our spiritual practices, healthy breathing can help to facilitate clearing the mind and opening the way to a deeper, prayerful experience.*

# 33
# Breathe

_Prayer Anchor:_ _"The spirit of God has made me, and the breath of the Almighty gives me life" (Job 33:4)._

There is a wonderful movie titled _"Ever After"_, a love story that I enjoyed watching. There is a scene in the movie where the character played by Drew Barrymore is about to make a grand entrance to meet the man she has fallen in love with. He does not know her true identity and this is the night she must tell him. She is dressed like a fairy princess and upon entering the ballroom where he is waiting with many guests looking on, she stands tall and says to herself: Breathe.

Did you ever have one of those kind of moments? A "just breathe" moment? When we are stressed, upset, angry or even overly excited it seems we don't breathe as we should. Our breathing is shallow and cut off. It's at moments like these that we must remind ourselves to breathe.

I don't know if they still do it in these days and times but when I had my children and probably when I was born too, the attending physician to a new born would first tap the new born baby on the bottom to help him/her catch that first breath with a big yell. It was to get the lungs operating and help the baby open up the throat area and start breathing. I remember the doctor saying to me that it is good for the newborn baby to cry (apparently it exercises their lungs and strong lungs can make for good, natural, healthy breathing).

There are healthy ways to breathe and unhealthy ways also. When we do not breathe fully we can cause stress to the body and mind. Poor breathing habits can contribute to illness and disease in the body. Unfortunately, unless we take a class that teaches us the techniques of healthy breathing, the only training we have had on proper breathing is that first tap on the bottom that the doctor gave us on the day of our birth.

237

**As part of our spiritual practices, healthy breathing can help to facilitate clearing the mind and opening the way to a deeper, prayerful experience.** There are workshops, books and tapes on the how-to's of healthy breathing. But for our purpose and this prayer practice, learning to breathe deeply and fully will help move you to the place of inner quietude that will enhance your prayer experience.

## *Prayer Practice*

Sit upright in a straight-backed chair. With both feet flat on the floor, hands resting lightly on your lap, consciously become aware of your breathing. Take your attention to the rise and fall of your chest. Breathe deeply and slowly. Inhale through the nostrils; exhale slowly through the mouth. Practice breathing like this until you fall into a rhythm. This should take you to a relaxed state. Relax and breathe. Continue to inhale through the nostrils, and exhale through your nostrils. Reflect on the scripture from Job: *"The spirit of God has made me, and the breath of the Almighty gives me life."* Relax even more, as you think the word "relax" and continue to breathe deeply and fully.

On the inhalation silently affirm: *"The spirit of God has made me,"* on the exhalation, silently affirm, *"and the breath of the Almighty gives me life."* When you are ready to conclude your prayer, fill your mind with thoughts of peace and harmony. If there is some prayer desire that you have, without addressing it, affirm gratitude for the right outcome of the situation. Remember, "Your Father already knows what you need before you ask him" (Matthew 6:8).

Continue to breathe and relax, open your eyes slowly, and remain in this peaceful state for as long as you can. Go about your business for the day with a refreshed spirit. Whenever you remember throughout the day, take a moment to relax and just breathe.

*When we open ourselves up to a personal vision from God, our receptivity is like a magnet that draws to us new possibilities.*

# 34
## Pray for a Vision

*Prayer Anchor:* "*Write the vision; make it plain on tablets, so that a runner may read it. For there is still a vision for the appointed time; it speaks of the end and does not lie. If it seems to tarry, wait for it; it will surely come, it will not delay" (Habakkuk 2:2-3).*

I have been consciously setting goals for myself for at least the last 20 years. I used what was called a "Goal Achievers Journal"[5] created by Jack Boland (my minister at the time). It has made a difference in my life since it forced me to have a vision for my life. Having a goal announces "where I want to go;" having a vision says "I can see myself getting there." We all should have a vision for our lives or at least for some aspects of it.

The Book of Proverbs is considered to be biblical teachings on wisdom. It is filled with instructions and guidance on how to lead and live life by making wise decisions and choices. One of those kernels of wisdom is. "Where there is no vision, the people perish" (Proverbs 29:18 KJV). The New Revised Standard Version of the Bible says it this way "Where there is no prophecy, the people cast off restraint" (Proverbs 29:18 NRSV).

Whichever version you choose to read, it is wise to have a personal vision. Without a vision we flounder from project to project, job to job, relationship to relationship, etc. We are not clear on where we are going, nor do we know where we want to go. Someone once said, "If you don't know where you're going, any road will take you there." Without some sense of where we're going or where we'd like to go, our day-to-day, week-to-week, month-to-month, and year-to-year activities are just that - activities. Consider the cat that chases its

---

[5] Currently this is called the Master Mind Journal, published by Renaissance Unity, Warren, Michigan.

tail. Lots of activity but it really doesn't go anywhere. Activity does not equal progress.

For most of my early work life, I was what I called a job-hopper. I started working when I was 16 and right out of high school. I would work on a job for two years maximum and then, something would stir in me and I had to move on. I would get bored and create some reason why I had to leave. Even after I finished college, two years on a job and then I was seeking some place else to go. Finally I thought starting my own business to share my talents would get me settled into one place. Well four years and two businesses later, I had a spiritual experience and made the move toward ministry.

After two years in my church in Miami, I started to feel uneasy, knowing my history. I wondered if I would create some grand reason to leave. But the real opportunity came after the third year. I was faced with a very good reason to leave - a few people wanted me to, and made it well known. For a time I thought this is it, my past has caught up with me once again, and I was mentally preparing to leave.

But what I had not counted on was a flash back of the vision I had been given for my life. When I took my ordination for ministry, I was given a vision of serving in a vibrant, spirit-filled ministry. So there I was 3 years in Miami with the opportunity to leave. I was face to face with a defining moment to either fulfill my destiny with more of my past, or a chance to embrace a new reality for myself.

I remember the night I sat in prayer and said something like "Dear God, lead me to the vibrant spirit-filled ministry where I am to serve." After sitting in the silence with this request on my heart for what seemed to be all of two minutes, an inner response came to me: "You are already there, stay."

Well I've been at the same church to date for 11 years. The turning point for me was personally realizing the power of vision for my life. Once there is a vision it helps to make the major and minor decisions we will be faced with in life. The vision becomes the litmus test by which we gauge and measure our choices.

Our vision may involve being the best we can be in our relationships with others, making a meaningful contribution to society through our careers, living healthy lifestyles, expressing personal spiritual growth in our lives, living lives of financial independence, or whatever speaks to our hearts and souls. **When we open ourselves up to a personal vision from God, our receptivity is like a magnet that draws to us new possibilities.**

In the book of Habakkuk, we are given key ingredients on receiving a vision from God. We must be willing to prayerfully wait for a vision from God within. The vision we want is a God-directed vision. We want the guidance, clarity and blessings of harmony and prosperity to unfold in our lives with ease and under grace. So we wait. If it seems to be delayed, we wait in prayer, meditation, and silence knowing that it will surely come. Habakkuk tells us to write it down. When we write what has been revealed, we bring clarity of thought to the vision we receive.

I often hear people talk about wanting to know their purpose. Purpose comes with a prayerfully discerned vision. In prayer we set our intention to be open to God's plan for our lives. When we prayerfully open ourselves up to greater possibilities for our lives, God's vision will surely come, and our purpose is revealed.

The process is three-fold: First, accept that there is a divine plan for your life; second, be open to letting it be revealed; and third, cooperate with the unfolding guidance as it begins to manifest.

First let's consider how we know there is a divine plan. I like the scripture that tells of Jeremiah's call "Now the word of the Lord came to me saying, 'Before I formed you in the womb I knew you, and before you were born I consecrated you; I appointed you a prophet to the nations' " (Jeremiah 1:4-5).

It is revealed to Jeremiah that his life was important and meaningful and was backed by a divine plan with a specific purpose. Before he was born, God had an idea which Jeremiah was brought forth to fulfill. This became his vision for his life. It is God-given and God-driven. The same is true for you me. Each one of us has been brought forth with an important and meaningful life, backed by a divine plan with a specific purpose. We pray a visioning prayer to gain access to the divine plan that is uniquely ours.

The second part of the process is being open. When it was first revealed to me that ministry was my purpose, I did not accept it. I was not open to it. It meant changes in my life that I thought I had to make on my own, and they seemed far beyond my reach and understanding at that time. I was resistant until many outer signs revealed themselves. I finally listened to the inner revelation. "If it seems to tarry, wait for it." The scripture warns us that sometimes we must be patient as the vision is revealed to us. The vision may seem delayed or we are not quite ready to embrace it. Either way, if we will stay committed to the prayer and follow divine guidance, the vision will surely be revealed, and we will be ready to receive it at the right time.

Third, cooperation is required on our part. So often we do not cooperate with God's good that has already been laid out before us. We may even indulge in self-sabotage and become the road block to our own demonstrations. "And if a house is divided against itself, that house will not be able to stand" (Mark 3:25). Sometimes we are like that house, working against ourselves by way of negative thoughts, fear-based decisions, as well as unproductive words and actions that do not support our own prayers.

Have a vision for your life. Find your purpose through prayer and meditation, and then live the life you were born to live.

## *Prayer Practice*

Several of the prayer practices mentioned in other chapters will help in this particular process. Fasting and silence will be very beneficial in drawing out that inner vision that God has put in your heart. Your role in receiving God's vision for your life is to prepare your mind and heart. This work is done through prayer, meditation, silence, and fasting. If it is possible set aside a 7-day period of focused prayer and fasting. If you could do this away from your home to avoid distractions this would be the optimal prayer situation. Find a retreat center that will allow you to keep silence. You may set a conscious commitment to fast from negative thinking and solid food for all or part of the 7 days as you desire. But give this life-changing experience all the focus and attention you can possibly arrange for it will be a time of great transformation for you.

Write out what comes to you in prayer. I have mentioned journaling in many of the prayer practices in this book and that is because I want to stress that it is important. Journaling is a tool to help you discern and assess the inner revelations that will assist you on your spiritual journey. And besides, Habakkuk said to "write the vision."

It will help to read some of the scriptures where vision is revealed in the Bible. My favorites are: Jeremiah, Joshua, and Nehemiah. Read Jeremiah chapter 1, Joshua 1:1-9, Nehemiah Chapter 1 and 2:1-8. Know that anyone who has received God's vision for their life, on some level of consciousness, they were open to it and prepared to receive it. On the conscious level of mind there may have been some resistance such as in Jeremiah's case, there may have been some fear such as in Joshua's case, but they did receive what God intended for them. Nehemiah fasted and prayed in response to his desire to make a difference and received the vision to rebuild the city of Jerusalem.

You may have some resistance or fear to overcome. But one thing we learn from reading about Jeremiah, Joshua, and Nehemiah: what is God-given is God-driven. "I hereby command you: Be strong and courageous; do not be frightened or dismayed, for the Lord your God is with you wherever you go" (Joshua 1:9).

In your prayer time,
- Know that the spirit of God in you wants you to know the vision for your life, so that you may live it and, to glorify God. "It is the Father's good pleasure to give you the kingdom" (Luke 12:32). It is your Creator's good pleasure to reveal to you that which you have been consecrated to be and do.
- Focus your attention on your heart as you imagine God's love for you so incredibly deep and strong that to reveal the vision

for your life is God's own act of grace toward you. Your act of love will be to receive it and then to set out being it.

- Get centered in God's presence. (Use your own words in prayer. This is the general idea. The more authentic your words, the clearer will be your revelation).
  - o Surrender your life completely to God. *"I surrender myself to you Oh God. I lovingly place all that I am before you."*
  - o Wait in silent meditation. *"In silence my God I wait for you. I wait that you may have your own way in me."*
  - o Ask inwardly that the vision for your life be revealed to you. *"I humbly ask from my heart, the soul of my being, that the divine vision for my life be made known to me with clarity, and under grace."*
  - o Spend time consciously bathing yourself with thoughts of gratitude and thanksgiving.
  - o End your prayer. *"Father, Thy will be done in and through me now. Thy will is my will."*

If you are committed to receiving God's vision for your life, be patient. It may take days, weeks or even months, but stay with it. Nothing will change your life more drastically for the better than discovering God's vision for your life or some aspect of it and then setting out on the awesome journey to live it.

*There is a time to be
in communion
with God,
where we speak
no words, our purpose
is to just be.*

# 35
# A Time to Keep Silence

_Prayer Anchor:_ _"For God alone my soul waits in silence,_
_for my hope is from him" (Psalm 62:5)._

The writer of Ecclesiastes said it best: "...a time to keep silence, and a time to speak..." (Eccl. 3:7). Yes in the prayer process there is a time to speak the word of Truth and know it is done. There is a time to speak our powerful affirmations and trust they are indeed making a change in our consciousness. There is a time to announce our intentions for our own benefit and the benefit of others. However, keeping silence has its place if we indeed want to grow spiritually. There is a time to listen inwardly. **There is a time to be in communion with God, where we speak no words, our purpose is to just be.** One of my favorite quotes by Charles Fillmore, the co-founder of Unity, is "All power has its birth place in the silence."[6] Being still and quiet, going within, so that we may have a conscious experience with God is one of the best prayer practices we could ever establish for ourselves.

In the first chapter of the Gospel of Luke, Zechariah learns the lesson and value of knowing when it is time to keep silent. Zechariah learns from an angel that his wife Elizabeth will bear him a son. Zechariah doubted this, after all he and his wife were beyond the age they thought it would be possible to bear children. When Zechariah spoke his doubts to the angel, he suddenly lost his ability to speak. His speech was restored after the child was born and about to be named John. After such a long time of silence, when Zechariah did finally speak again, he was filled with the Holy Spirit and his first words were words of praise to God.

To keep silent for 9 months must have been difficult, but it gave Zechariah an opportunity to find that inner connection with God, to

---

[6] Charles Fillmore, _Talks On Truth,_ originally published by Unity School of Christianity, 1901 NW Blue Parkway, Unity Village MO 64065. www.unityonline.org

contemplate his relationship with God and to listen inwardly. It is not a surprise that when his speech was restored, that he was filled with the Holy Spirit. He also spoke of a prophecy that he had received. He announced the coming of a Savior for whom his son John would pave the way. Wow! This is the power of silence.

Keeping silence is more than the absence of talking. It is being in silent communion with the God of our being. In our prayer anchor, the Psalmist describes that experience: "For God alone my soul waits in silence, for my hope is from him." All that we could ever hope to manifest is from God within. To gain the full value of an experience with God, we must go to the place within where we speak no words, we listen, just listen. There is no pleading our case to God, no explaining what we want, no affirmations, just surrender, stillness, being, listening and silence.

### *Prayer Practice*

Give yourself the gift of a silent retreat. Decide on the number of days. If it's your first fast, start with 24 hours. After you've got that first one under your belt, you'll want to expand to 3, 7, 10 perhaps even more. You can schedule your retreat alone or organize one in your spiritual community. Find a quiet retreat center that is conducive to silence. You don't want to have to order your food or talk to the staff or anything. There are many places to go for this kind of retreat. Find one and just do it.

If you are not able to get away, or just as a maintenance prayer practice, between silent retreats, you may intentionally set a full day aside when you can be in the silence from your home. Arrange your environment so you will be without interruption.
- Turn off the phones.
- Watch no television.
- Do not listen to the radio or read the newspaper.
- Stay away from places where people may engage you in conversation. In fact, plan your day or days so that you will not have to go out in public.

250

Let this be a time of contemplation, prayer, inner reflection and the enjoyment of being.

In your time of meditation you might begin by using a favorite scripture or scriptures throughout the day.

Psalm 62:5 really captures the essence of what a silent day might incorporate: "For God alone my soul waits in silence, for my hope is from him." If you want to add a little more spiritual power to your silent time, try fasting from solid foods on liquid juices and lots of water. Journaling during this time can also be very revealing.

After your day of silence, the answers to questions you did not even know you had may surface. New ideas may come to you with ease. You'll feel relaxed and at peace.

It is very helpful to establish a day of silence as a regular prayer practice. When I was in ministerial school I took a day of silence each month. Now I take for myself a silent day once a quarter and then a 3 - 7 day silence when I am on sabbatical from my church in the summer. Once you experience a silent day, or a few days of silence, you'll wonder why you didn't do it sooner. "Be still and know God" (Psalm 46:10).

Note: When you do an extended silence, anything over a few days, take time to transition back into your normal life; do it gradually. You will be working with Spirit on a very deep level during your time of silence. Immediate return to lots of busy-ness and lots of outer activity may feel harsh to the gentle, peaceful consciousness you've experienced during your silence. Be gentle with yourself on your return.

By following whatever guidance God reveals to us during this process, we are blessed beyond just the demonstration.

# 36
## Make a Covenant with God

*Prayer Anchor: "Then Jacob made a vow saying, 'If God will be with me, and will keep me in this way that I go, and will give me bread to eat and clothing to wear, so that I come again to my father's house in peace then the Lord shall be my God, and this stone which I have set up for a pillar, shall be God's house; and of all that you give me I will surely give one tenth to you'" (Genesis 28:20-22).*

As we read the scriptures we see that God made a covenant with several figures in the Bible; there was Noah, Abraham, Isaac, David, and others. In our prayer anchor, however, we see Jacob being the initiator of the Covenant with God. Jacob was not doing anything that was outside the realm of what God desires from any of us. A covenant is a binding agreement between two parties. It is synonymous with a promise, pledge, contract, etc. In his covenant, Jacob took 5 steps: 1) he acknowledged God's presence, 2) he asked God to guide him, 3) he recognized God as the source of what he needed to be sustained, 4) he asked for God's help in overcoming his errors, and 5) he committed to put God first in his life and affairs.

Jacob was following God's lead by setting in place the covenant relationship that had already been established with all human kind. "This is the sign of the Covenant I am making between me and you and every living creature with you, a covenant for all generations to come" (Genesis 9:12).

God has already made a covenant with you and me. That covenant is the quality of life we get to live and influence by following the spiritual laws our Creator laid out for us before we took bodily form. In making a covenant with God we acknowledge that we are ready

255

and willing to accept this sacred relationship with God in creating the circumstances of the life we desire.

Once, when I introduced this idea of making a covenant with God in a workshop, one of the participants firmly objected saying that God does not make deals. After which she stood up to leave, apparently thinking she would not finish the workshop.

I asked her to consider that God works in our lives by spiritual principles or spiritual laws. She agreed to this. I pointed out to her that when we make our covenant we are simply saying we commit to working with the spiritual laws that are in place for our use. We agree to do our part, so that God working in our lives as divine law, can do the rest. When we make our covenant with God, we set an intention to work with God in balance with the law of giving and receiving. We want to receive and so we are willing to give. No deal, just working with the spiritual laws of life rather than against them. We must remember that God works through us, rather than for us.

When we make a covenant with God we are not bargaining with God, but rather we are making a conscious commitment to deepen our relationship with God. We acknowledge the method and means to do this is in partnership with God. "With God all things are possible" (Matthew 19:26). We are saying that we are ready to take God up on the promise "it is the Father's good pleasure to give you the kingdom" (Luke 12:32). We're also saying we have knowledge of and accept that "the measure you give will be the measure you get back" (Luke 6:38).

**By following whatever guidance God reveals to us during this process, we are blessed beyond just the demonstration.** Our relationship with God is strengthened and expanded to a new dimension. Whatever we can do to increase our relationship with God is not bargaining but rather it is an opportunity for a new level of spiritual growth.

The covenant is made in two parts. In part one, we follow Jacob's example and state clearly that which we are asking God's help in accomplishing. In part two, we state that which we are willing to do for God in gratitude for what we have asked and, with our faith, expect to receive.

Those who want something for nothing may have a difficult time with this. Part of our personal growth comes when we abandon the error belief that God should give us what we want without any accountability or responsibility. God is our source of all we could ever want and manifest in our lives. We make this acknowledgement not for God but for ourselves. We need to know where our source is and how to access it and claim it.

A covenant is an example of what it means to "seek first the Kingdom of God" (Part II of the Covenant) and all these things shall be added unto you (Part I of the Covenant). (Matt: 6:33).

## *Prayer Practice*

### Making the Covenant

1. Prayerfully clarify your desires and then list them on a sheet of paper titled "My Covenant with God"; this is part one. This is our official prayer request. Be as specific as you can but leave room for Spirit to work. End your request with "this or whatever is for my highest good."

2. For part two, prayerfully ask God's guidance on what to give in return for the desire you have stated. Spend time in prayer waiting for divine guidance. Your part will always be to do some kind of service. Always make tithing part of your commitment in the covenant. Jacob demonstrated his acknowledgement of God as his source by vowing to give a tenth to God's work. Along with whatever else is revealed to you in prayer and meditation make giving and sharing your time a part of your covenant with God.

3. Sign your covenant as you would any other agreement and date it. This is important. It shows you are making the partnership agreement with a serious intention to do your part. When we set an intention, we mark in consciousness that it is done, and so it will be.

257

4. Read your covenant daily. God will work through you to take care of Part 1 while you work on Part 2. Stay open to new opportunities and possibilities. God works in wonderfully awesome and sometimes mysterious ways.

# Part Six

# Prayer Practices Simply for the joy of living

*In the scriptures,
we find that singing
was a natural form of
prayer as well as an
automatic response to
answered prayer.*

## 37
### *Make a Joyful Noise*

*Prayer Anchor:* *"Make a joyful noise to the Lord, all the earth. Worship the Lord with gladness; come into his presence with singing"*
*(Psalm 100:1, 2).*

Singing has been an important aspect of worship from ancient times. The Book of Psalms is a collection of prayers that were mostly expressed through music and sung as part of the worship experience. Today we continue to sing songs of praise, thanksgiving, celebration, and joy during formal worship services. But this is a spiritual practice that we do not want to overlook as part of our individual prayer experience.

Throughout the scriptures, we see Bible characters singing their prayers, praises and songs of thanksgiving. Moses sang a victory song after God led Israel out of Egypt. Deborah and Barak sang a song of praise to God after a battle ended in victory for them. David sang many songs of praise and thanksgiving. Mary sang a song of praise to God for conceiving Jesus; Zechariah sang a song of praise for God's promise of a son and Solomon sang songs of love. And the list can go on. The point is we have seen singing modeled over thousands of years as prayers and as expressions of gratitude to God for answered prayer. Its longevity as a spiritual practice tells us it is a powerful method of praying and praising God.

**In the scriptures, we find that singing was a natural form of prayer as well as an automatic response to answered prayer.** When we sing a song of praise it is difficult to be sad. When we sing songs that have a positive message we feel inspired. Singing can help us to heal our minds and bodies. Singing can help us find inner strength. Singing helps us to express our joy.

Singing can be a positive method of praying depending upon the words we sing. There are songs particularly in secular music that do not affirm the goodness of life, love, peace, honor, and respect for others. Even so, they act as prayers also. The spiritual laws of life are no respecter of person or circumstance. Negative words in a song activate the law of mind action just as the positive words of a song do. The law of mind action simply says that we create our outer experiences by the thoughts we hold in our minds. When we sing, we hold thoughts in our minds that will produce the outer experiences we hold when we sing negative or positive words. For this reason, we must watch the songs we sing and the songs that our children sing. Let the words we sing be uplifting. Let the law of mind action work for you to help create the life you desire. Let the words we sing be words that glorify and praise God. "Praise the Lord! How good it is to sing praises to our God; for he is gracious and a song of praise is fitting" (Psalm 147:1).

When we add the vibration of music to positive, life-affirming words, we magnify their ability to reach deep within us. Singing has such an emotional and soul-stirring range that it can bring us to tears of joy and tears of sadness all in the same song. If we set our minds on singing as a regular spiritual practice, we will discover the benefits are powerful prayers that have the capacity to heal the body, lift the mind, and fill the spirit with joy.

## *Prayer Practice*

Incorporate any 1, or all 3 into your personal prayer time:
- Begin your prayer time with a song.
- Sing a song as your prayer.
- Close your prayer time with a song.

Find songs whose words inspire you, lift you up, make you smile, make you laugh, stir your soul with hope and faith. These are the kinds of songs you want to make a habit of singing. To get a quick lift during the day or to infuse a bit of inspiration at just the right moment, sing a song of praise and thanksgiving.

Find songs that say the kinds of words you would say in a prayer. You may consider a hymn that you like and sing it as it is, or create your own words to the tune of a familiar hymn. I have a little jingle I sing to myself to the tune of Amazing Grace. It is especially meaningful for me and I am inspired whenever I sing it.

Every chance you get to sing in a worship service, sing up, sing out and sing with authority. Remember you are praying the words of that song, so give it your full voice and the same sincerity you would any prayer you pray. Sing often and sing from your heart.

Since this singing is for you and the God of your being, don't worry about how well you sing. God cares about your heart and your intention, so make a joyful noise to the Lord as often as you can.

*If you truly want
to prosper in all
that you do, think big.
You can have money
and sooooo much more.*

# 38

## Prosperity

**Prayer Anchor:** *"Their delight is in the law of the Lord, and on his law they meditate day and night...In all that they do, they prosper"* *(Psalm 1:2-3).*

When I was a young girl growing up in Detroit, I did not know that there were spiritual laws governing prosperity. I rather thought I was to grow up, work very hard on a job (that I would hopefully like), get paid as much as I could, and claw my way up the ladder of success. It was not until my adult years that I heard in a Unity Church that there were laws that governed how we may live a healthy, happy, and prosperous life. Since that time, I have made it my life's mission to learn and live the laws that govern a blessed, well-lived life. I rather feel like the Psalmist in our prayer anchor: I delight in the law of the Lord.

For those of us who delight in the law of the Lord, we find joy in living the best God - centered life we can. We are conscious that we have a part to play in our own destiny. We make it our business to read, study, and learn the spiritual laws that govern life. We desire to know them beyond what we get from the Bible, books, preachers, and teachers. We invest time in prayer and meditation, day and night to understand and discern God's will for our lives. We discover that the more we delight in the law of the Lord, we begin to flourish, grow, and prosper. We read the words, "In all that they do, they prosper" and we want even more to know God and the laws that govern this great potential we have to prosper.

If we are not experiencing the level of prosperity that feels right to us, our prayer anchor tells us what to do. And, it makes the point, that the work is ours to do. The rules of engagement have already been laid out for us as the spiritual laws that govern all spiritual matters. When we learn the rules, live by the laws, we gain access to the rich consciousness that allows us to prosper in all that we do. Once we move beyond the consciousness that is trying to get God to give us something, as if it were being withheld, we can begin to accept the abundance that God has already prepared for us through spiritual laws.

For the past few years in our church in Miami we have done a Millionaires' series based on the books by Catherine Ponder. One year in attempting to demonstrate how we are all millionaires, I handed out a form "You are God's Millionaire." It was an assessment form asking each person to give a dollar value to our many intangible assets like faith, love of family members and friends, personal creativity, level of humor and so on.

It was a revealing exercise. It proves to us that we have so much to be grateful for and that the value of our life is certainly worth more than a million dollars. This is important to note, because prosperity is so much more than money. And even still most of us are a lot more prosperous than we give ourselves credit for. Prosperity includes all that is important for us to enjoy a sense of well-being. We are prosperous to the extent that we have:

- Faith in something larger than our personal selves.
- Health (mind and body).
- Peace of mind.
- Loving companionship of family and friends.
- Freedom of self-expression.
- Positive self-esteem.
- Dreams, desires, and goals we are working toward.
- Money to use and enjoy.
- A sense of humor.

Assess your life to determine the level at which you are experiencing the qualities above. Do you have a strong faith that inspires you to expect good to come your way? What level of health, peace of mind, harmonious relationships are you experiencing? What level of self-expression and positive self-esteem do you enjoy? Do you have money to meet your needs with plenty left over to enjoy the life you desire? Do you laugh a little or a lot?

270

The extent to which you are satisfied with these areas of your life is the degree to which you are experiencing prosperity. Prosperity is seeing life from a larger view. When we limit prosperity to just money, we are thinking small and that is a poverty mentality. A poverty mentality places limits on our ability to enjoy the fullness of life.

When we discover that life is great, grand, and awesome, we enjoy expressing our part in it as great, grand, and awesome. To think prosperity is to think big. It is more than money, more than things. It is a life of possibility, celebration, hope, and a dynamic consciousness of God. It is creative self-expression, fun, health, joy, peace of mind, compassion, beauty, and even more. **If you truly want to prosper in all that you do, think big. You can have money and sooooo much more.**

## *Prayer Practices*

In your time of prayer acknowledge God as your source *"God is my source of all good."* This is a Truth that must be the foundation for our prosperity. Say it, write it, sing it, whatever it takes to get this major Truth into your thinking and feeling nature.

Next make of list of that which God has provided for you in your life. List everything you can think of. Example: I start my list with *"God has provided me with a heart, lungs, teeth, blood, sight, hearing, a mind, etc, etc."* After you have written such a list (and it should be long), Place a dollar value on that list. In other words, how valuable is what God has already provided for you?

Now list those areas in your life where you would like to see some enhancements. For example if your health is not what you would like it to be at the present time, you may include it as a prosperity prayer. I don't have to tell you that this does affect your prosperity: Doctor bills, prescriptions, time from work, the mental stress, tests, etc. Construct your prayer around your desire to prosper in the area of health, beauty, and well-being. You may alter this prayer or use one that speaks to you. The underlined section is where you customize your specific desire.

*"I delight in my awareness that God is my source. This truth is the law upon which I focus my thoughts, words and actions. Every day, morning and night I am conscious of God as my source and supply; I think it, I speak it, I meditate upon it. <u>I prosper, and my health is strong and perfect. I prosper and my mind is at peace. I prosper and I feel great in mind and body.</u> I delight in the grace of God working in and through my life and affairs. In all that I do, God's ever constant stream of grace flows in me, and I prosper."*

Support your prayers by reminding yourself that you are prosperous – you have a lot going for you already. Frequently take a look at your long list of what God has already provided for you. Surely God did not provide all those blessings to abandon you now or ever. Use your faith, use your truth, use your awareness that God is your source to take you to the next level of enjoying the life that you desire.

True prosperity is lived on a daily basis; it is not just something we pray about when we want something. Here's how you may keep your prosperity flowing in all areas of your life on a regular basis:

- Have a daily routine of spiritual practices, and do them 'religiously'.
- Be a generous and cheerful giver.
- Keep the energy around you harmonious.
- Take some time to enjoy the outdoors.
- Schedule fun time for yourself.
- Maintain harmonious friendships.
- Spend quality time with family.
- Find a place to volunteer your time and talents.
- Take good care of your physical health with exercise and a healthy diet.
- Forgive quickly.
- Keep your thoughts positive.
- Acquire some practical knowledge on money management principles and put them to work in your affairs.
- Practice love, compassion, honesty, and integrity in your interactions with others.
- Never stop growing and learning.

All of these areas can affect our ability to experience life as great, grand, and awesome.

Here are some additional ideas to support your ongoing expression of prosperity:

- Be mindful to occasionally wear colors that represent wealth and prosperity like purple, green, red, deep blue.
- Light a green or purple candle from time to time as a conscious reminder of the light of prosperity that flames in you.
- Sing songs with lyrics that remind you that you are healthy, wealthy, and blessed.
- Keep a gratitude journal with entries on how grateful you are for your prosperity.
- Pray with a prayer partner or partners who support you in your goals, dreams, and ideas for increased growth and prosperity.
- Keep your home and living environment free from clutter. Allow your home to be your castle.

*David was not just celebrating for God, David was celebrating with God.*

# 39
## Dance the Prayer You're Praying

**Prayer Anchor:** *"David danced before God with all his might..."(2 Samuel 6:14).*

I have enjoyed dancing since my teen years. I was never very good at it, but I enjoyed it so I kept trying and continue to love it to this day. The freedom to be me was my attraction to dancing. I feel the music and just move. "What fun! So several years ago when I read in the Bible that David danced, I became interested in dancing as a spiritual practice, in addition to the fun I had doing it.

I could relate to David's desire to dance. He was celebrating a major accomplishment. The Ark of the Covenant was finally being returned to be placed in Jerusalem. David was filled with joy and could not help but express his gratitude by moving to the music. The scripture says he "danced before God." David had done a good thing according to his understanding of God's will. As a leader, he wanted what he believed was best for the people of Israel. The Ark of the Covenant was their national treasure, and now it was in their possession after 100 years. Surely this was cause for David to celebrate, and he chose to dance before God, and I believe with God.

David wasn't just dancing so that God would know of this gratitude; he was having a dance with God to fully acknowledge the joy of such a momentous accomplishment. **David was not just celebrating for God, David was celebrating with God.** He was praising God with every move, giving thanks with his mind, body, and spirit. I rather believe that God enjoyed dancing with David by the evidence that afterwards David enjoyed a long period of peace and continued prosperity.

Many indigenous cultures enjoy dance as part of their religious and spiritual practice. Many years ago, my daughter became interested in West African dance. I was not so interested in it at the time, but then I discovered that they were not just dancing for the sake of dancing

277

which is certainly fine, but that the dances had themes; many of them were prayers of thanksgiving, celebration and setting an intention for their desires to manifest.

I rather think that my daughter "danced before God." As she was dancing in a West African dance recital, she met the man who she would marry a year later and who would be the father of her first child and my first grandchild. She had been praying to meet the man she would fall in love with and marry. Her career was intact, and she felt ready to be a mother and was praying that she would marry someone who would also be ready to have children.

One of the many dances she performed that night was a dance that was a "mating dance." In many parts of West Africa the women who are ready for a mate, dance with intentional movements and a made up mind to attract a mate. So they dance and dance and dance. I can say that it worked. She and her husband are very happy, and my grandson is an angel.

Now it may not be your prayer request to attract a mate, nor is that my point in telling you this story. My point is that the principle of engaging body, mind, and spirit toward a single idea with focus and feeling is a very powerful energy to harness in any endeavor. Yes, my daughter did other prayer practices toward her desires and dancing was just one of them. But I dare say the dancing helped to condition the consciousness to receive the divine right answer to her prayer.

## *Prayer Practice*

Dance your prayer. Whatever kind of dance that works for you is fine. Set a mental intention as to what the dance means to and for you. Fix your prayer request in your mind and let your spirit feel the music as you engage your body in motion. Let yourself feel free to express. Stretch out of your comfort zone; try bold purposeful moves. If your prayer is worth dancing for, it is worth consciously expanding the avenues by which your guidance may come.

Whatever you are praying for or about may require some courageous actions you have not yet been willing to face. Dancing helps to practice being fearless through the act of trying new movements. Dancing helps the mind, body, and spirit to act intentionally and deliver results. Isn't that what we all want our prayers to do – deliver results? When we dance our prayers, we give ourselves permission to let the body move freely and unencumbered so that we shed apprehension. We break out of the box of self-consciousness so that we are more open to the good that we desire.

The gift of engaging your whole being in the prayer is to follow through on any guidance and divine ideas received. You'll be anchored from a place of fearless receptivity - you'll be willing to try new things that perhaps you did not consider before.

Ask around. There are places where you can learn to do what is called "spiritual dance," liturgical, or even African dance. The principle is the same: Engage the mind, body, and spirit in your prayers and expect powerful results.

Dance, Dance, Dance! Any kind of dance will do. It's a great way to lighten up, have some fun and exercise the body all at the same time. So pray while you dance, and dance while you pray!

*If you want rest and relaxation, you will have to plan it.*

# 40
## *"Go Apart and Rest"*

*Prayer Anchor:* *"Come away to a deserted place all by yourselves and rest a while" (Mark 6:31).*

You may not think it needs to be said, but it does: Take time for yourself to rest and relax. This is something I'm sure you already do. However, just as Jesus knew the disciples needed to hear it, and then do it, so do we need to be reminded of it. We should not take lightly the importance of good self-care through rest and relaxation.

In the story from our prayer anchor, the disciples had been on a very busy and full schedule. They were off doing God's work and had little rest and took little time to eat, or nourish their bodies. Being the teacher that Jesus was, he gave them a lesson in self-care. He wanted them to know the importance of getting away for a while to relax and replenish their spirits. And so Jesus took the disciples away to "a deserted place" so that their rest would not be interrupted and so that they could "rest awhile."

With the busy lives many of us lead, it is easy to put our time for rest and relaxation off until tomorrow or next month or next year. Answers to the questions we often seek in prayer come to the mind that is free of clutter and busy-ness. This prayer practice is just a wonderful reminder to schedule some uninterrupted time to be alone and to catch up on your rest and relaxation.

When we let our physical body feel the stressful effects of busy-ness and long to do lists, it affects our ability to receive divine guidance and inner wisdom with mental clarity. When we are exhausted physically our thinking process is not as keen, our minds are not as sharp. We simply don't make our best decision and choices when the body and mind are not at their best.

Our ability to consciously become aware of Spirit in prayer can be impeded by our physical and mental exhaustion. Many years ago when I was learning to meditate, I learned a great lesson. During the

283

class I was taking to learn meditation I kept falling asleep. I would try again at home in the evening before going to bed and the same thing would happen. I did not understand why I could not stay awake, for I really wanted to learn to meditate. I finally told the meditation teacher of my difficulty staying awake. He asked me a few questions about my daily activities and as I told him what my busy days were like he finally interrupted me and said "stop, stop, stop, you are falling asleep because you are tired, it's that simple. Get some rest, and try your meditation first thing in the morning in small portions of time 15 -20 minutes". Well, he was right. I never even realized that it was my exhaustion that was the problem, not my technique.

So, whether it's soaking in a relaxing bubble bath, taking a walk on the beach, watching a sunrise or sunset, sitting in your lounge chair, listening to music, reading a book or just doing nothing you must take the time to catch your rest. Do the things that will allow you to relax your mind, body and spirit.

Caution: Do not think that your vacation is necessarily a time when you will get to rest and relax. **If you want rest and relaxation, you will have to plan it.** In today's times traveling can be work. Sometimes we pack in so many activities in our travels that when we return home we are exhausted from our vacation. Schedule some real rest time when you are vacationing, balance activity with time to relax.

## *Prayer Practice*

Look for ways that you can combine your relaxation techniques with your prayer practices. For example, if you enjoy watching sunrises or sunsets, plan a time of prayer to the view of the sky. If you enjoy taking a bubble bath, do so as you think on God, the beauty of life, gratitude, words of praise and thanksgiving. The key to getting the most from this prayer practice is to relax first, then incorporate your prayers into your mode of relaxation.

284

Use some of the other prayer techniques mentioned in this book to enhance the relaxation mood like lighting some candles, putting on some relaxing music, or burning some essential oils in your diffuser.

Your prayers will be more effective if you take a moment to relax your mind and body. Make relaxation one of your tools for a successful and blessed prayer and meditation experience.

- Mentally set aside all of your worries, fears and anxieties.
- Focus your attention on your breathing for a few moments.
- Visualize yourself in a peaceful scene or setting, and slowly say to yourself over and over again: *"relax."* Do this until you do feel more relaxed.
- Affirm: *"I am now rested, relaxed, and receptive to experience the presence of God in me. I rest in the spirit of God in me. I relax in the spirit of God in me. I am receptive to God expressing in and through me as peace, life, love, and wisdom."*
- As you continue to relax, pray whatever prayer desire is on your heart.
- Close your prayer with a statement of relaxation and gratitude such as: *"I now relax and go about the activities of my day. I trust and know that my prayer has been heard and is answered with ease and under the graceful hand of God. With gratitude on my heart and in my mind, I let it be. Amen!"*

You will find that if you approach prayer relaxed and worry-free, you will enjoy the process of being in communion with God (which is nourishing to the spirit), and divine ideas will easily find a resting place in your mind.

And, finally, at least once a year, take a spiritual retreat. It can be a day or two, but longer is better. Give yourself the gift of renewal. Let your spirit be refreshed and nourished by celebrating your spirituality with rest and relaxation.

Enjoy!

*A grateful heart
and mind becomes a
mighty magnet drawing to
itself more to be grateful
for.*

# 41
## *Raise your Gratitude Quotient*

*Prayer Anchor:* *"Give thanks in all circumstances; for this is the will of God in Christ Jesus for you" (1 Thessalonians 5:18).*

Some folks seem to be naturally grateful in all circumstances. I was in awe of the attitude of a young man I met years ago, who at the age of 25 had been in a car accident leaving him paralyzed and confined to a wheel chair. He always had a smile on his face; he was polite to others; he was grateful for whoever picked him up for church and saw that he was returned home; he loved to sing and always had something fun and funny to say. He was truly a unique example of being grateful in all circumstances.

However, for some of us an attitude of gratitude must be cultivated. Once we begin to let ourselves practice being grateful, it grows on us and in us. We make a discovery about gratitude that we would not otherwise know: Gratitude is magnetic. **A grateful heart and mind becomes a mighty magnet drawing to itself more to be grateful for.**

I've kept a gratitude journal for many years. When I finish one, I start another. I list what I am grateful for, and most days I list ten things. Other days I list just a few. Gratitude is a part of my regular prayer practice and it is a must for anyone who has a commitment to on-going spiritual growth. We literally raise our gratitude quotient when we develop an attitude to "give thanks in all circumstances." The higher our gratitude quotient, the more magnetized we are for the gifts of health, happiness, joy, peace, love, and prosperity.

The fact that it helps us see ourselves and others in a more compassionate way is another added bonus. When I am grateful for, as our prayer anchor says, "all circumstances," I find something to be grateful about in whatever I am facing. If I am in a difference of

289

opinion with someone, I find it easier to forgive myself and them if I focus on finding something to be grateful for in the experience.

An attitude of gratitude can be developed over time if practiced sincerely and on a regular basis. When we pray, remembering to be grateful for whatever the results are to our prayers, we are forming a habit; and habits are not easily broken, negative or positive. So, why not form the positive habit of being grateful?

When I was a child, my mother often had to coerce us kids to eat our vegetables at meal-time. She would make us say grace over our meal and tell us to be grateful for whatever food was before us. She instructed us to eat what was in front of us even if we didn't like it. She told us it would still nourish our bodies even if we didn't like the taste of it, and for that nourishment we should be grateful. So we ate the carrots, broccoli, string beans, and all the vegetables Mom placed before us, not for the taste, but for the nourishment (and because Mom said so). It was always a great joy on the rare occasions that for eating all of our vegetables Mom would reward us with dessert. To eat my Mom's peach cobbler was more than worth eating a few carrots and string beans. It was that good! So we learned to be grateful for whatever was before us and hold on to the hope and the expectation that something good can follow when we are indeed grateful for what we already have "in all circumstances."

## *Prayer Practice*

When you pray, start your prayers with a statement of gratitude. For example: *"I am grateful for all God's blessings in my life"* or *"Thank you, God for my life and all the good that continually flows to me for my use and enjoyment"* or *"Gratitude fills my mind and heart and I am a magnet for even greater blessings in my life and affairs."* Make your own statement, but do make gratitude part of your prayer.

Remember how Jesus prayed before raising Lazarus from the dead: "Father I thank you for having heard me" (Luke 11:41). When we are thankful, even before the outer demonstration, it is an indication of an attitude of gratitude. Praying with gratitude as a theme will help in expanding your consciousness toward greater blessings.

You'll discover that you have much more to be grateful for. Your level of inner confidence will allow you to trust that you can overcome whatever experiences come your way. You'll know that you won't face any situation alone. God is love and we live in that love. "It is the Father's good pleasure to give you the kingdom" (Luke 12:32).

End your prayers with statements of gratitude. In fact vary your methods by making your whole prayer a series of statements. Express your heart-felt gratitude for the good you are now demonstrating and the good you expect to demonstrate.

I suggest that if gratitude is an area where you know that you need strengthening, begin right away by listing 10 things each day for which you are grateful. Do this for 21 days. Nothing is too large or small or insignificant to place on your gratitude list. The important thing is to do it consistently until it becomes second nature to look for the good in your life and in your experiences. This will help to raise your gratitude quotient and the attitude shift toward thanksgiving will bless your affairs in new and exciting ways.

*The desire for companionship, friendship, and partnership is our soul's craving for an awareness of our connectedness with our Creator.*

# 42
## Love and Romance

_Prayer Anchor:_ *"Love is patient; love is kind; love is not envious or boastful or arrogant or rude. It does not insist on its own way; it is not irritable or resentful; It does not rejoice in wrongdoing, but rejoices in the truth. It bears all things, believes all things, hopes all things, endures all things. Love never ends... When I was a child, I spoke like a child, I thought like a child, I reasoned like a child; when I became an adult, I put an end to childish ways. For now we see in a mirror, dimly, but then we will see face to face. Now I know only in part, then I will know fully even as I have been fully known. And now faith, hope and love abide these three; and the greatest of these is love"* (1 Corinthians 13: 4-8,12,13).

The desire for intimate love is a natural urge within us. **The desire for companionship, friendship, and partnership is our soul's craving for an awareness of our connectedness with our Creator.** That soul urge is often imitated by our human relationships with each other. Service, creativity, charity, mercy, and intimate partnerships are all soul urges by which we long to experience and express the love of God. No matter how we express the love of God on life's journey, the important thing is that we do, for our soul longs for it.

We are love beings. God created us from love for love. The love of God exists within each one of us. In its natural state, it is always ready to express, grow, and thrive that we might radiate it from one to another. Love is within us and all around us even when we don't see it or feel it. Yet, when we speak of love and then add romance to the discussion, the discussion can take as many turns as there are people on the planet.

295

Though love is something most of will admit we want, and something we already have to some degree, it is one of the areas that is still perplexing to many of us. Our experiences that have shaped our human reactions to love are varied and our perspectives are enormous: Some of us seem to be in love with life; some fall in love easily and quickly; some are afraid to be loved; some worship love's imitations; some have no time for love; some find love in the simple joys of every day life. So what is love, loving and being loved? We could study many aspects and types of love, but we would eventually be led back to: Our soul's hunger for an awareness of our connectedness with God.

Life is filled with lessons on love, loving and being loved. But from the spiritual point of view, all love is Self-love. The love that many of us spend a life-time searching for is but our need for the awareness that God is love, and that God is within us. "God is love, and those who abide in love abide in God, and God abides in them" (1 John 4:16). Love is God loving Itself in and through us. "God lives in us, and his love is perfected in us" (1 John 4:12).

So our work is to love God, love ourselves and love others. The good news is that this is all one in the same life lesson. "You shall love the Lord your God with all you heart, and with all your soul, and with all you mind.' This is the greatest and first commandment. And a second is like it: 'You shall love your neighbor as yourself'" (Matthew 22:37-39).

When we claim ourselves to be "loving and romantic," we have positive self-love – we love God and we love ourselves. The doors to our hearts are open, with a genuine invitation for opportunities to let God love through us. With this high level of love going on in us, we can say we have a consciousness of love. Love and romance is going on inside us all the time. It is a romance with life itself. To love God, ourselves, Life and others, is all one in the same effort and a dynamic expression of true romance. We are romantic for the sake of expressing the pure joy that we exude. This romance causes us to smile a lot. We can laugh at ourselves and at the sometimes amusing twists and turns we find along life's journey. We are romantic because we are love in action. We live the moments of our days filled with an awareness of love's magnificence.

I use our prayer anchor for this chapter a lot when I perform a wedding ceremony. Although the apostle Paul reportedly wrote 1 Corinthians 13 to show how we must love others, we can use the same ideals to begin to meet our inward need to know and experience God's love. In the Prayer Practice for this chapter, I make the suggestion that you write 1 Corinthians 13 in your own words with your own personal meaning. Following is an example:

> "If I speak in the tongues of mortals and of angels, but do not have love, I am a noisy gong or a clanging cymbal. And if I have prophetic powers, and understand all mysteries and all knowledge, and if I have all faith, so as to remove mountains, but do not have love, I am nothing" (1 Corinthians 13:1-2).

No matter how eloquent the words I speak, no matter my spiritual gifts of seeing into the future and knowing of many things that others do not, no matter how strong my faith, with all these things to my credit, if I do not love myself, I really have nothing at all. If I do not have love in my heart as the foundation for all that I am, there is a void within me that cannot be filled with all my knowledge, faith and eloquent words. If the door of my heart is closed I have cut myself off from the goodness of God.

> "If I give away all my possessions, and if I hand over my body so that I may boast, but do not have love, I gain nothing" (1 Corinthians 13:3).

I will not stray from love's gentle blessings by the glitter of material things. My wealth has its foundation in knowing God's love for me. I gain everything I could ever hope to acquire from the love of God constantly filling my heart, mind and soul with the consciousness of peace, health and prosperity.

> "Love is patient; love is kind; love is not envious or boastful or arrogant or rude. It does not insist on its own way; it is not irritable or resentful; it does not rejoice in wrongdoing, but

rejoices in the truth. It bears all things, believes all things, hopes all things, endures all things" (1 Corinthians 13:4-7).

Others may judge my innocence harshly, believing me to be unwise and unschooled in the ways of the world. But I smile at this assessment, for I know that patience and kindness can harmonize the toughest challenge. I understand what those who judge me do not. My time, talent and energy are not well spent on qualities of irritability, resentfulness and rejoicing in the trying times that others face. Love bears the tears and the joys of my days. Love believes the best is always unfolding for me regardless to the outer appearances. Love hopes in the face of hopelessness. Love will endure beyond any experience I can ever have. Should my human heart ever feel broken and sad, even then, Love will bring me back to itself, whole and perfect.

> "Love never ends. But as for prophecies, they will come to an end; as for tongues, they will cease; as for knowledge, it will come to and end. For we know only in part, and we prophesy only in part; but when the complete comes, the partial will come to and end" (1 Corinthians 13:8-10).

There will be many ending places along my life's journey. With all the insight I have into what should be, according to my limited understanding, it is not a sufficient match for the power I gain when I am firmly grounded in God's love. Love has no end. Love is the completeness, the wholeness I searched for in former days. But God's steadfast, everlasting, enduring love is my sufficiency. And now that I know the power of love actively expressing in and through me, I rejoice and celebrate Love today, and into eternity.

> "When I was a child, I spoke like a child, I thought like a child, I reasoned like a child; when I became an adult, I put an end to childish ways. For now we see in a mirror, dimly, but then we will see face to face now I know only in part; then I will know fully, even as I have been fully known" (1 Corinthians 13:11-12).

In my past, I was ignorant of love's power. I spoke, thought and reasoned that it was not wise to love in all circumstances. I had a list of excuses for not giving myself over completely to love's magnetic pull. Now, as I live in a state of grace I am aware that God is the ruler of love, and God's own way of loving is in and through me. I have put aside my former ways of ignorance. I remember in former days when I looked in the mirror, I could not see my own beauty glowing with the radiance of God's love. I searched outside myself to change the picture in the mirror before me. But now whenever I pass a mirror I see the love of God looking back at me. I now know what it feels to see love vibrant and alive, face to face. I understand fully that I am one of the many, beautiful faces of God's love.

> "And now faith, hope, and love abide, these three; and the greatest of these is love" (1 Corinthians 13:13).

Yes, I remain faithful. My faith is stronger and deeper than ever before. My faith is in the power of God expressing in and through me now and forever. Yes, I am filled with hope. My hope does not waiver from God's power to heal, bless and prosper any experience as I turn within to ask, seek and knock. My hope is in the promise of the goodness of God showing itself forth in my countenance, my spirit and my soul. And yet, with all my faith, with all my hope, Love stands out in a bold and brilliant image I have for myself. I have discovered God is love, and that God is within me. I have discovered the love I have been seeking was always within me. I am Love!

Whether your desire is to deepen the love you feel for yourself or to make a harmonious love connection with another, the place to begin your work is within. There are many books that you may read to learn of outer romance techniques. However, in this chapter, I offer you the spiritual principles to not just have love and romance as a possession, but to be the essence of love and romance all your days, for "Love never ends."

When our soul's urge is toward greater love in our lives, we should consider these principles:
1. Our desire for love is the inner thirst to express the love of God from within.

2.  We can only give what we have, and we receive according to what we give.
3.  Our outer relationships reflect some aspect of what is going on within us.
4.  Our overall attitude toward others reflects in the quality of our relationships.
5.  Healthy self-love is a magnet for a healthy relationship.
6.  The relationship that is most important in shaping the quality of life that we live is the one we have with ourselves.

Our loving Creator has given us the power to choose how love's story will play out in our lives. Isn't that exciting! We get to use the laws of life to create our own "love story." There are many avenues you may take to fulfill your dreams, however, a spiritual foundation will enhance your experience of love whether you choose to be in an intimate relationship with another or choose to enjoy a healthy romance with yourself, while creating and living the life that you desire. The choice is always yours, and to love is the greatest choice of all.

## *Prayer Practice*

**There are 4 parts to this prayer practice.**
- Part 1 of the practice is to develop a greater awareness of God's love within. Work with 1 Corinthians 13 in 21-day increments. When you are reading this scripture it is the love between you and the God of your being. Take the time to write the scripture with your own interpretation, one that has significance to you. After 21 days, take a break from it and go to Part 2.
- Part 2 is to select one focus area according to your desire: A) Expand your own level of self-love; B) Increase love and romance in your current relationship or marriage; or C) Attract a love relationship.
- Part 3 will help to anchor into your consciousness in the work you have done up to this point.
- Part 4 is to live your life as the love being you've become.

**Here are some general affirmative statements that may be used at any time:**

*"I am in Love with Life and Life is in love with me. I am living the great romance of all time – it is with life itself. This great romance is my all sufficiency in all things. I can never lack for love, I am Love."*

*"I find great inner strength, poise and peace as I express the power of love in me."*

*"Love guides my way in all that I think say and do."*

*"I am the expression of divine love and joy-filled romance."*

*"I love myself."*

*"I am love in action."*

*"I am so filled with divine love that I radiate it wherever I go and in all things that I do."*

*"Every person that comes into the range of my consciousness will be aware of divine life, love and wisdom as my very essence."*

*"The love of God expressing in and through me, is a drawing power to my right and perfect mate."*

*The love of God expressing in and through me heals me now". (You may substitute the word "heals" with prospers, blesses, guides, etc.).*

*"I am a love magnet."*

*"God is Love, I am Love."*

*"I am loveable, loving and loved."*

**Part 1:**

Morning Prayer: Meditate on the words from 1<sup>st</sup> Corinthians 13 for 21 days. Center your thoughts on the scripture sentence by sentence. Meditate on the words as the one being loved by the presence of God in you. Each morning of the 21 days, spend time working with the scripture in ways that allow you to experience being loved and loving. Write out what the ideas expressed mean to you. Let your mind be so filled with thoughts of love, that you set the tone for your day as a powerful expression of peace, harmony and joy. Let love influence all that you do for the day. Notice opportunities during your day to live from a loving space; to truly live the scripture. Let love awaken in you and in your daily affairs and interactions with others.

Evening prayer: Just before bed, read the scripture aloud 3 times before going to sleep. This will allow your subconscious mind to go to work on your love vibration while you are asleep.

Incorporate some of the other prayer practices discussed in this book along with this prayer. Light a white candle symbolizing God's unconditional love. Then light 2 pink candles (the color that gives off the vibration of love) 1 pink candle for your human expression of love and the other for the higher expression of love that you desire. This symbolizes a unification of self taking place within you. Orange blossom incense is great to burn during this process.

**Part 2:**

    **A) To expand your own self love:**

Meditate on Psalm 139: 1-18 daily for 21 days. Meditate on the words line by line in your morning meditation. Read it aloud at night just before going to sleep. Journaling during this time will be very helpful. You may uncover areas where you have been blocked. Once these blocks are revealed, they can be healed.

*Note: Take extra care with yourself during this time. Be especially good to yourself, more than usual. Make a conscious and intentional effort to spend time pampering and nourishing your spirit.*

**B) To increase love in your marriage or relationship:**
If your partner is open to this, read from the Song of Solomon together. Take a chapter each night and read it to each other just before going to sleep.

If your partner is not willing to read it with you, then read chapter three on your own daily for 21 days.

*Note: During this time also read some books on the subject of putting more romance in your relationship. Reading the scriptures will help build up the inner love and romance consciousness, but you will want to apply the outer romantic experience also.*

**C) To attract a love relationship:**
For 21 days, read from the Song of Solomon. First read it through in its entirety over several days and then chapter 8 if you are a woman, chapter 7 if you are a man.

Read it aloud; meditate on it before going to sleep at night. Again engage the subconscious mind to get involved in this desire you have to attract love into your life.

*Note: If you have been without a partner for a long period of time, consider reading other books that will allow you to ready yourself in attitude and outer appearance.*

## Part 3
Go back to 1 Corinthians 13, this time praying it for another 21 days. Write the scripture in your own handwriting and read it once daily. Use white paper for self love, pink paper if you are already in a relationship and yellow if you are attracting a relationship. If you sincerely completed Part 1 and Part 2, your love consciousness has been expanded and this step will help you to anchor love into your very essence as you affirm the words in the scripture daily.

## Part 4
Go forth and be the love consciousness you have established for yourself. Let your thoughts, words, and actions express the love that you are. The Law of Love has been activated by you, in you. It will

respond with your continued attention to being loving and loveable. Let your love light shine.

Incorporate other prayer practices in this book along with this one. Have fun being loving, loved, and lovable.

*Whenever you give a blessing, you set a cause in motion for a blessing to be returned to you.*

# 43
## The Power of Blessing

_Prayer Anchor_: _"With it you shall anoint the tent of meeting and the ark of the covenant, and the table and all its utensils, and the lampstand and its utensils, an the altar of incense, and the altar of burnt offering with all its utensils, and the basin with its stand; you shall consecrate them, so that they may be most holy; whatever touches them will become holy" (Exodus 30:26-29)._

As a minister, I have been asked to bless many things. From rings to cars, purses and wallets to sacred objects, books, business proposals, pens, pets, new jobs, businesses, - all come to mind off the top of my head. Nothing is above or beneath being blessed. I was even asked once to bless a teddy bear. Allow me to share that story.

A young man wanted to give a Valentine's gift of a teddy bear to his adult girlfriend. Apparently, she had never owned a teddy bear as a child and she grew up under a difficult childhood. He thought a "special" teddy bear would soothe some of her childhood hurts that she continued to carry; he wanted to be able to tell her that the teddy bear had been especially blessed for her. I don't have to tell you that the teddy bear made a tremendous hit with his girlfriend. I have since been told that she treasured that gift more than any of the others she received for many years that followed.

Our prayer anchor tells of the Old Testament preparation for worship procedures. Every item to be used in conjunction with worship had to be anointed and blessed. Everything! The ancients were very strict about the treatment of what was considered sacred. They were convinced that good, positive energy was important in worship, ritual, and everyday situations. The utensils, the lampstand, the altar, the basin were all anointed with special oil. Each piece was consecrated to be a blessing in support of the worship experience.

The idea is that objects hold energy that has been conferred on them with high spiritual intention. Our minds are powerful and as spiritual beings we have been endowed with the ability to confer a blessing or to pass a blessing on from us.

When we bless, no matter what we bless, we set a vibration of increased good into motion with our words. Jesus blessed five loaves and two fish and it increased to the point where over 5000 people were fed. Our words are powerful, particularly when we give them the intention to uplift, increase, and multiply. At the last supper, Jesus blessed the bread and the wine on the table. Today people take communion to receive their portion of the blessing Jesus handed out two thousand years ago.

As children many of us were taught to bless our meal before we ate it. We confer a blessing on the food before we eat it for several reasons. First, we are grateful to receive the nourishment to our body. We know that the body needs nourishment and so we are grateful to have what we need in sustenance. Second, we bless the food to confer that it is indeed the essence of nourishing energy to fulfill the nutrition requirements for the health and well being of our minds and bodies. Third and finally, we confer a blessing of thanksgiving on the hands that prepared the food as a representation of our gratitude for the time, love, and willingness of the preparers.

In my mother's house as a child we also had a 4$^{th}$ item to add to our blessing before the meal. We were required to confer a blessing on the dishwasher. Now back in those days the dishwasher was not a machine, it was one of us kids. After the meal one of us would have to wash a sink load of dishes that had fed anywhere from 5-10 people, plus the commercial size pots and pans that my mom used to prepare the meal. So, we always closed our meal blessing with "and thank you God for blessing the dishwasher."

Blessing is a part of our religious and spiritual culture. We say "God bless you" when someone sneezes. I often hear "Bless your Heart," or "Have a blessed day." The fact is that we like to confer a blessing to others as a kind gesture, as an invocation of the multiplying power of our words, or as an expression of gratitude. But there are ways in which we turn the idea of blessing upon ourselves - by blessing what we do and by blessing what we wear.

In early chapters in this book we've covered the notion of blessing what we do and where we go. We bless the day before us with our morning prayers; we bless our journey to our workplace as we leave our home; we may even bless the other drivers on the road; everywhere that we go, we bless the path before us.

The very clothing we wear should also be blessed. Think for a moment – have you ever had a "lucky suit" or a "lucky dress?" You may not have said the words as a blessing but by believing it was "lucky," you have blessed it with a title that means extra special good things happen for you when you wear that item of clothing. Is the item really blessed with the ability to help draw good experiences to you? Yes! You are the one who set the mental intention in your mind that it carries "good" energy, and so it does.

Do you remember the story of Queen Esther? She had a mighty task before her. What did she do before going to the King to make her request? "On the third day, when she ended her prayer, she took off the garments in which she had worshiped, and arrayed herself in splendid attire. Then majestically adorned, after invoking the aid of the all-seeing God and Savior...She was radiant with perfect beauty, and she looked happy, as if beloved..." (Esther 15:1-5, Apocrypha). She prayed and put on her "blessed" attire. Who could say no to someone that is "majestically adorned" after having invoked God's blessing and, someone who glowed with radiant beauty, looking happy? Certainly not the King. Esther received what she asked for.

Bless the clothing that you wear. Adorn yourself as God's Queen or King. Let your inner beauty radiate from you and reflect in the outer garments you wear. Have you ever noticed how good you feel about yourself when you are well dressed? You radiate confidence and positive self-esteem. When the prodigal son returned home, the first thing his father said was "Quickly, bring out a robe - the best one - and put it on him; put a ring on his finger and sandals on his feet" (Luke 15:22). He wanted his son to claim the consciousness of prosperity and well-being. He wanted his son to feel the blessing of knowing his true royal birthright.

It has been said that "clothes don't make the man," and that is true. But we've heard that the clothing of movie stars and famous people from history can be sold for thousands of dollars at an auction, just because that person blessed the clothing by wearing it. You are a child of God and you have the power to name what you wear as blessed and have it be so. "So out of the ground the Lord God formed every animal of the field and every bird of the air, and brought them to the man to see what he would call them; and whatever the man called every living creature that was its name" (Genesis 2:19).

From the top of your head to the soles of your feet, you can name all that adorns your body "blessed," and expect great blessings to be drawn to you, conforming to your word, which brings me to shoes. I like shoes. Sometimes I shop for them without buying any. I like looking for them and looking at them. Shoes speak to me. Sometimes when I am shopping for them they call my name. I try them on, and if they feel as good as they look, they are mine. I'm often told that I wear cute shoes. That's because I do. I have set in my mind that I wear cute shoes, and so it is true for me. I bless my shoes. Yes, I bless my shoes. Not because they are cute but because shoes cover my feet and my feet take me where I want to go.

I have a constant prayer that everywhere I go I am blessed and a blessing to others. My feet move me where I need to go to do the things that are mine to do. I am grateful for my feet. I reward my feet by adorning them with cute shoes. "As shoes for your feet put on whatever will make you ready to proclaim the gospel of peace" (Ephesians 6:15).

The idea with all this blessing of everything is so that we develop a consciousness of blessing everything and praising God in all circumstances. This is how we are prayed up all the time. "Let everything that breathes praise the Lord! Praise the Lord" (Psalm 150)! **Whenever you give a blessing, you set a cause in motion for a blessing to be returned to you.** If you name something as blessed, it will indeed respond to what you call it. "Whatever the man called every living creature, that was its name" (Genesis 2:19).

## *Prayer Practice*

Take every opportunity in your day to confer a blessing. When you come in contact with others, give them a silent greeting: *"God is blessing you now."* When you pass an accident on the highway, send a blessing to those involved: *"The light and love of God bless you now."* When a friend comes to mind, send them a blessing wherever they are. If you thought of them, they may well need a blessing at that particular moment.

Let your words be words of power going forth to bless others and honor the gift that God has given us to name our blessings.

Compose your own spirit-guided blessings. If you are blessing something tangible and it is present, touch it as you are giving the blessing. If you are not able to touch it physically or if it is an intangible idea, use your power of visualization to bring it into your consciousness.

The following is a general blessing format you may use: *"In the name and by the power of the Holy Spirit in me, I name you _____.* Fill in the blank with the blessing you choose. Then, define or clarify what the name means to the particular context in which you confer the blessing.

- If you were blessing your favorite business outfit before an important meeting: *"In the name and by the power of the Holy Spirit in me, I name you 'Blessed for Success!' As you adorn my body this day, you conform to my word and exude wisdom, harmony, peace, and prosperity for overflowing success in all that we experience this day."*

- If you were blessing the pen by which you expect to sign a major business deal: *"In the name and by the power of God in me, I name you 'Blessed with Wisdom!' The work that is ours to do this day is done from the wisdom of Spirit and all is well."*

- If you were blessing a new wallet you just purchased: *"In the name and through the power of Christ in me, I name you 'Blessed with Money Substance!' You are the keeper of the rich substance of money supply now pouring in as abundance, and flowing out in balanced, wise and generous proportions."*

- To bless the new job you have just been hired for visualize yourself walking up to the new workplace and affirming: *"In the name and through the power of Jesus Christ active in my consciousness now, I name this new job 'Blessed in all Ways!' In all that is mine to do, my way is blessed with health, happiness, success, and prosperity. The talents and gifts I lovingly share are a blessing to anyone who comes into the range of my consciousness."*

A consciousness that blesses everything all the time is the heavenly state of consciousness we all deserve and surely desire. Daily practice and commitment will help us attain it. God Bless You!

# Part Seven

# Prayer Practices that move you forward for new opportunities

*This is one of the prayers that, when answered, thrusts us into a deeper relationship with the God of our being.*

## 44

# The Ultimate Prayer of Service

*Prayer Anchor: "Jabez called on the God of Israel, saying, "Oh that you would bless me and enlarge my border, and that your hand might be with me, and that you would keep me from hurt and harm! And God granted what he asked" (1 Chronicles 4:10).*

This prayer is one of the most powerful that I know. Many people report having been blessed beyond their wildest imaginings after praying this prayer. This is the prayer to pray if you want God to bless you and "enlarge your border."

What kind of blessing was Jabez asking for? Was he asking for riches, fame, honor, the respect of others? What did he mean by "enlarge my border?" What was Jabez really asking God to do?

More importantly, what are you asking if you indeed decide to pray the prayer that was so successful for Jabez? What is the true blessing that you are seeking? The long and short of his story was that Jabez prayed asking God to bless him, and God answered his prayer. That's all we know. So we would do well to have a clear understanding of what we are asking before we engage such a powerful prayer.

Jabez wanted the blessing of a close relationship with God. The privilege of having God use him was the blessing he sought. Did he receive riches, fame, honor, and the respect of others? The scripture does not tell us. But we know Jabez did form a close relationship with God, one where God's hand was upon him and kept him from hurt and harm. That was his prayer, and that is what he received. This close relationship with God found Jabez positioned to access all the riches, fame, and honor one could desire, if that had been his intention. We can be sure that as Jabez served God, he did not live in lack or want. We know Jabez had the respect of others, for his story is short, but worthy of being in the Bible.

To pray that your border be expanded is to pray for an expanded consciousness of service to God. When you ask that your border be enlarged, you are asking God to give you greater responsibility in some divinely selected area of service. When your border is enlarged, opportunities will come your way that will stretch you to a higher level of your potential. The prayer of Jabez clearly asks for God's special blessing with which comes greater responsibility, new opportunities to serve, and tremendous spiritual growth.

**This is one of the prayers that, when answered, thrusts us into a deeper relationship with the God of our being**. Our personal answer to the prayer of Jabez will call for a commitment from us to do God's will with whatever is revealed. We will need to surrender our personal will to the larger picture that God has for our lives and the lives of those whom we will serve.

Several years ago I decided to try the prayer of Jabez for 21 days. I prayed it 3 times each day for each day during my chosen period. It was not long after praying this prayer, that one of my colleagues asked me to consider running for our Regional Executive Committee of our International Association. I had been asked to run the year before and had declined the opportunity. But because I had prayed the prayer of Jabez I knew that yes was to be my answer. I was elected and I have joyfully served on that Committee for several years now. I have enjoyed the opportunity to be of service to the ministries in our 8 State Region. Had it not been for my serving in this capacity, I would not have had the opportunity to meet the people I have had the chance to know and love. It was and still is my prayer that I have brought a blessing to the role in my earnest desire to be of service. The bottom line is that my border (my area of responsibility in some divinely selected area of service) was indeed enlarged as a result of this powerful prayer.

Now I said that I had been asked to run for the Committee the previous year. What made the difference? I have no doubt that praying this prayer contributed to opening my consciousness and

318

preparing me for new opportunities. My "border" was expanded; that translated to a new level of willingness in me to gracefully and joyfully accept greater possibilities to be of service. That is the power of this prayer.

The prayer of Jabez is one that we pray unselfishly. I call this prayer the ultimate prayer of service. When we pray this prayer, our first concern is not for ourselves but with the desire for God to use us. This is the prayer that gives God the invitation to give us something great, grand, and awesome to do that will benefit others. The gift is that no matter what opportunities are presented to us as a means of answered prayer, God's hand will be upon us, guiding us every step of the way, smoothing out any crooked places and any rough edges. The spiritual growth we will sustain from this close relationship with God will cause us to be blessed in every area of our lives.

Pray this prayer sincerely when you desire to invite the Spirit of God to use you in service to others. You will receive an answer that will allow you to witness the power of an earnest prayer. Your part will be to stay open to opportunities presented to you, and to follow the inner guidance that Spirit is sure to reveal. This prayer is often prayed by those who are seeking to know their purpose and a strong desire to know God's will for their lives. Many have been blessed by this short but powerful prayer. It is indeed the ultimate prayer of service.

## _Prayer Practice_

Pray the prayer from 1 Chronicles 4:10. Affirm it with your whole heart and with all the sincerity you feel about serving God. Meditate on the words. Set your intention to pray this prayer daily for as long as it takes to receive your assignment from God. You may also give yourself a time period in which to pray the prayer such as 21 or 40 days. During this process, know that Spirit is working on your behalf, and your job will be to stay open to receive the guidance clearly and then to follow it.

You will notice the movement of Spirit as you affirm this prayer. So stay open to opportunities that come to you. Notice that you will be invited to do things that you had not necessarily considered before. Notice the ideas that come to you for your consideration. Pay attention to the people you come in contact with and note the kinds of things they say to you and ask you to participate in.

Jabez knew that to serve God was indeed a great blessing. As you pray this short but powerful prayer, great blessings will come upon your life and your border will be expanded beyond what you have imagined.

*In our times of prayer, we have the power to set in motion a vibration that moves toward building peace, compassion, and unity in our collective consciousness.*

# 45
## Pray for World Peace

*Prayer Anchor:* *"All the nations will be gathered before Him, and He will separate them one from another, as a shepherd divides his sheep from the goats. And He will set the sheep on His right hand, but the goats on the left. Then the King will say to those on His right hand, 'Come, you blessed of My Father, inherit the kingdom prepared for you from the foundation of the world: for I was hungry and you gave Me food; I was thirsty and you gave Me drink; I was a stranger and you took Me in; I was naked and you clothed Me; I was sick and you visited Me; I was in prison and you came to Me.' "Then the righteous will answer Him, saying, 'Lord, when did we see You hungry and feed You, or thirsty and give You drink? When did we see You a stranger and take You in, or naked and clothe You? Or when did we see You sick, or in prison, and come to You?' And the King will answer and say to them, 'Assuredly, I say to you, inasmuch as you did it to one of the least of these My brethren, you did it to Me."* (Matthew 25:32-40 NKJV).*

My mother had eight children. Growing up, our house was always filled with activity. There seemed to be disagreements all the time between us kids. But Mom wouldn't stand for fighting among us. She took a firm stand about it. It didn't matter who started it, who passed the first lick or who said the first provoking word. Both parties involved in the fight were punished, because as Mom said, both should know better than to try to solve any problem by fighting. She had a no tolerance rule toward fighting.

But I remember one of the rare occasions when Mom allowed a fight between my sister and me to continue until we had tired ourselves out. At the time I didn't know why Mom allowed the fight to go on that day. She stood and watched the whole thing. If we got too close to something that might break, she would move it out of harms way or gently nudge us in another direction. But she let us fight to the finish. There was a part of me that wanted her to stop the fight, not just because I was losing terribly to my older sister, but after a while I was going through the motions and wasn't as angry about the situation as when we started, I was just trying to defend myself. After what seemed to be an eternity for me, the one who came in second place, we finally just stopped. Mom had us get cleaned up and then asked us both to sit with her on the sofa. She asked us who won and my sister proudly acknowledged that she had won. "What did you accomplish by beating on your little sister?" My sister about age 11 at the time replied, "I don't know, but I did win."

She had us hug and make friends again. We both were punished for fighting - the winner and the loser. We never fought again. We argued a lot. But we never took a hand to each other again. To this day, we are not just sisters, we are friends. Remembering this story reminds me of the words of Abraham Lincoln "I destroy my enemies when I make them my friends."

Using my mother's approach to looking at two parties fighting whether we talk about siblings, nations or all relationships in between:

- First, they should both know better. When we consider that 95% of the world's population is reported to be affiliated with one of the world religions, and that most religions have a teaching related to what we call the Golden rule, both parties should indeed know better. "In everything do to others as you would have them do to you; for this is the law and the prophets" (Matthew 7:12).

- When two parties use physical force against each other, what does the winner really gain? My sister succeeded in beating on me, but by her own admission she did not know what had been accomplished. It is the same for all relationships where

324

solutions turn physical. We could ask ourselves, "Does the 'winner' ever really win, when the method is violence?"

- Finally, when both parties realize that they are punished by their own participation in the fight, it just makes sense to find other ways to settle disagreements.

As we grow on our spiritual journey we discover a few cold, sometimes hard, facts about peace in the world or the seeming lack thereof:

1. If we are not experiencing peace in our home, community, nation, it is because the individuals involved do not have inner peace.
2. If we want to change the outer demonstration of violence in our world, the first place to start is in our individual inner world. Peace begins within the mind and hearts of individuals and reflects into our outer world.
3. The place to start is with ourselves. We can permanently change our actions from violence to harmony by first changing our thoughts and words.
4. What we do to another we do to ourselves, we are all one. The barriers that separate us are human made illusions.

As we discover that peace does begin within us, we begin to express it more in our lives. We learn the awe-inspiring lesson that there is a divine and intimate connection between happiness and inner peace. We can then take a stand for peace by choosing peace over error messages of prejudice, judgment, fear, and ignorance toward others. "Let us then pursue what makes for peace and for mutual upbuilding" (Romans 12:19).

We all look forward to the day when we will travel the world and feel safe. We all want to be treated fairly and kindly no matter where we are or where we are going. We all want to feel that our loved ones are safe to travel anywhere in the world. "How very good and pleasant it is when kindred live together in unity" (Psalm 133:1)!

The goal and desire is for all God's creations to live together in harmony and unity. And yet the question could be asked "If 95% of the world's population claims some affiliation with a religion, why can't we all seem to get along"? What has all this "religiosity" gotten us? It is difficult to believe we're all so religious and still treat each other so poorly.

In the summer of 2005 when Hurricane Katrina devastated New Orleans and other cities through which she passed, the outpouring of compassion was beautiful to witness. In devastating times, acts of charity seem to come easily for us. But between tragedies we still have much work to do on ourselves as a human race and as individuals. "If it is possible, so far as it depends on you, live peaceably with all" (Romans 12:18). When peace lives in enough hearts as ongoing compassion and kindness, we will be proactive in our move toward peace, and harmony will be the order of our days. **In our times of prayer, we have the power to set in motion a vibration that moves toward building peace, compassion, and unity in our collective consciousness.** If we are truly on a spiritual path, peace is on our prayer list.

## *Prayer Practice*

In your time of prayer, light a white candle as the flame of peace shinning light into the places where ignorance, prejudice and injustice appear. Say your prayers of peace, harmony, and joy to the world. Read sacred writings and scriptures that speak of peace on earth, peace among humankind, compassion, and unity. The prayer anchor for this chapter is a powerful scripture that invites compassion into our hearts. Make it a part of your personal prayers to expand your mind toward greater kindness and compassion.

Visualize the planet as a place where the golden rule is lived no matter what our religion, race, nationality, sexual orientation, primary language, geographic location or anything that seemingly separates us.

Spend time meditating on peace within first and then on the outer. Surround your loved ones, your community, city, state, country, and the planet with thoughts of peace, harmony, and unity. Take time to pray for world leaders that they are divinely guided in the choices that they make. Pray that we may all not just talk about the golden rule but that we live it and be an example of it for our children.

Here is a method you may incorporate into your prayers for world peace. Say the following prayer for each of the 7 continents. Light a candle for each continent as you begin to pray for it. You may use a map to identify the continent on the map as you pray, if not, just hold a vision of white light around the planet as you pray for each continent.

Fill in the name of a different continent each time you pray this prayer until you have prayed for all the 7 continents on the planet: Africa, Asia, North America, South America, Antarctica, Australia, and Europe.

*"There is one reality in the Universe, and It is the presence of God. The Infinite Heart and Mind of God is perfect peace. There is no place where God is not. The peaceful presence of God is fully present everywhere, all the time expressing as life, love, and wisdom. Throughout the continent of _____, God's perfect plan of peace and harmony is awakened in the hearts and souls of all living forms. _____, in the name and through the power of the Holy Spirit, I pronounce you the living testimony of peace, prosperity, wisdom, and compassion, now and forever more. The planet is now aglow with your light: Shine on _____; Shine bright! You are the light of the World."*

*When we love ourselves enough to let go of what is finished and complete, we discover that endings are really signals that new beginnings are available, possible, and ready to manifest for us.*

# 46
## Letting Go and Moving On

*Prayer Anchor: "The dead man came out, his hands and feet bound with strips of cloth, and his face wrapped in a cloth. Jesus said to them, "Unbind him, and let him go" (John 11:44).*

As we journey through life, we find ourselves in places where we must let go of what is complete so that we may embrace our next level of growth. Letting go can be a challenging experience depending on what we are faced with releasing, our ability to accept endings, and our willingness to begin anew.

Some of us must really work with ourselves to let our endings unfold gracefully. The good news is that there is a way to have graceful endings and welcome the fresh new beginnings of our lives. If we are willing to draw on our own inner strength and move forward one step at a time, we can face our endings with poise. New beginnings can be smooth and sometimes exciting.

Like anything else that we face on the journey, it's our perception and view that shapes our experience. Endings and our ability to accept them stem from the many attitudes that we hold about ourselves, life, and others. Attempting to hold on to that which is beyond our control and obviously finished is a setup for suffering. The question I have about suffering is, "why do it?"

Our method of releasing and letting go comes back to love as many things do. **When we love ourselves enough to let go of what is finished and complete, we discover that endings are really signals that new beginnings are available, possible, and ready to manifest for us.** When we really love what is finished, we are able to let it go for its higher purpose to be fulfilled. We may tout that "we like things the way they are," or "we don't want things to end," and yet recognize that endings are a necessary part of our own growth and spiritual development.

331

Some endings test our faith in God. Some endings leave us bitter and angry. Some endings bring up emotional pain that lasts long enough to devastate our lives and affairs. This is one of the reasons that it is important to have a spiritual philosophy on how life works. If we can think spiritually toward our times of letting go, we will not only "go through" our endings, we will "grow through" them.

Our spiritual understanding will help us through an ending that appears not to be in alignment with our perception of good. Our test then is to know and trust that nothing happens outside of divine order and that God is omniscience, the power that is all wisdom and all knowledge. Nothing happens outside the sphere of God's love, power, and wisdom. This may not be an easy concept to embrace when we are in the midst of what feels like a devastating loss. But this is also the reason we do not wait until we have a loss to develop and work on our own spiritual understanding.

As we face a tough ending we might do well to ask ourselves:
- Do I believe the grace of God is a continual presence of divine love in me, no matter what I'm experiencing? Even if I am hurting now, can I hold on to my belief that God's love is present in me and in the midst of my situation? Do I believe that God's love is a healing presence in my life?
- Do I have faith in God's law of divine order at work in this situation?
- Do I think that with my human personality, I know better than the all-knowing power of God?
- Do I really love myself enough to let go of what is finished and complete rather than holding on to that which represents pain and perhaps suffering?

Ask yourselves these and other questions to determine your receptivity to letting go. When we are receptive to facing what is complete from inner strength, we will move through our endings with integrity, dignity and ease and create the opening for everyone else involved to do the same. If your answers reveal that you are not open to letting go, rather than suffer silently, get some professional help. Talk to a counselor, therapist or a spiritual practitioner to help you sort through your feelings and prepare to move on. In the process of letting go of what is complete, you will discover inner strength that will empower you for the new experiences that are to come.

Let's face it, when we must let go of what is finished, it doesn't matter whether we are consciously ready to let go or not. Sometimes we have recognizable clues that the end is near and sometimes not. Some endings just happen - with or without our conscious instigation. It may show up like the transition of a loved one, divorce, children leaving home for college, friends moving to another state, being released from a job, and so on. There are times when we must exercise our ability to let go and let God guide us through what comes next.

The writer of Ecclesiastes had these words of wisdom to share: "For everything there is a season and a time for every matter under heaven" (Ecclesiastes 3:1). In a long list of occurrences he lists "a time to see, and a time to lose; a time to keep, and a time to throw away" (Ecclesiastes 3:6). Most of us probably don't like thinking of our need to release as "a time to lose or as a time to throw away," but as a metaphor it is quite appropriate. To lose or throw away is to cast off from ourselves that which is complete in some way, to let go with the knowledge that it is finished, to accept that what we are releasing is no longer ours to hold on to physically and emotionally. I did not include mentally and spiritually, because there are some parts of what is being released that we may want to hold on to, and we can find reassurance by holding on. The memories that are pleasant and uplifting and comforting to keep are always our right and our choice. In our spiritual evolution, whatever contributes to our growth is always with us in consciousness.

We must throw away our old attachment to what is finished and discover a new connection with what we are releasing. We don't need to release the pleasant memories only our attachment to the painful ones. Often our inner pain is around the circumstances of experience causing the need to let go, such as divorce. The marriage may have been good for many years, so those are the memories we may want to keep. However the divorce itself may have brought out the worst aspects of the marriage and the people involved. What we want to release then is the pain of the difficult breakup. We want to release the human tendency to get stuck in the "ending" aspect of what may once have been a good relationship and a beautiful marriage.

While we don't necessarily like knowing it, events have their own course to run and when they are finished, ours is to accept it and keep moving forward. Life unfolds in this way, life grows in this way, life is this way. Our job is to trust that the process of grace is perpetually unfolding in every situation. God has created a divine order to the unfolding of life and we cooperate with it as we keep moving toward a greater awareness of the power within us to overcome whatever challenges we face. We learn to let go of what is finished and move on. We learn to cast off the pain, keep the best of what is left, and begin to start anew.

In our prayer anchor, we find Jesus bringing Lazarus back from the dead. He spoke words of release by telling those at hand to untie Lazarus, free him from bondage, and let him go on his way.

Our prayers of release would be the same. We speak the word to release ourselves from the bondage that binds us to the past so we may grow forward to the good that awaits us. There are also those times when we must release others from bondage in our minds. Sometimes we hold on to people, wanting to keep them and the circumstances we enjoyed with them the same. Yet it may be their time to move in another direction for their highest good.

Sending my son off to kindergarten that first day was tough. In the midst of his big day he was excited, but I felt a bit of sadness in the midst of my joy. Our relationship would change, and I did not feel ready for it, but it was time. The day he packed his belongings and I drove him to college was another tough time. In the midst of his big day he was excited, but I felt a bit of sadness in the midst of my joy. Our relationship would change, and I did not feel ready for it, but it was time. And then I gave my daughter away to be married, and yes, that was tough also. It was her big day she was all grown up, beautiful, excited on a gorgeous summer day, but I felt a bit of sadness in the midst in my joy. Our relationship would change, and I did not feel ready for it, but it was time.

These were all lessons in letting go. Sometimes we are not consciously ready to make the changes that are before us, but change is a part of life, and in life, we must learn to let go when it is time. All relationships go through changes of some form. In every change there is a need to release the way things were and the opportunity to create the way things can be. We make it easy on ourselves when we do the releasing part gently and then expect and plan to create great new beginnings.

## *Prayer Practice*

Determine the level of your need to release and move on. The method you choose from what is listed here should be judged by you according to the level of release work you need to do. The level of release work will not be the same for releasing your child to go off to college, as it will be for a very painful divorce, or what you perceive to be the untimely loss of a job that you enjoyed.

Pray the general prayer listed below. The last two sentences of the prayer represent two scripture verses affirmed in the 1st person: 2 Timothy 1:7 and Philippians 4:13. You may want to write the scriptures in your journal. Next, start with the **Outer Releasing activities to support the inner work of letting go.** If deeper work is required, i.e., you are still having difficulty embracing the changes in your life, move to the **Inner releasing methods for inner work of letting go and moving on.** Choose them 1 at a time and if need be move to another as you feel guided.

**General Prayer. Take this prayer 3 times daily for 7 days.**

*"Through the power of God at work in me I have the strength, wisdom, courage, love and power to embrace the change that is before me. I place my trust in the unfolding of divine order and know that all is well. I let God guide my way and the way of everyone involved in this change. I let my faith lead the way to new found ways*

335

*of joy, peace, happiness, and fulfillment. For God did not give me a spirit of cowardice, but rather a spirit of power and of love and of self-discipline. I can do all things through Christ who strengthens me."*

## *Outer releasing activities to support the inner work of letting go.*

There are several things we can do to facilitate the prayer process of release. It is helpful to do some outer releasing along with releasing emotional and mental states of consciousness.

1. This is the time to clean out the closets and clean our drawers that have become cluttered. If we are releasing a relationship, it may be time to take down photos particularly if the ending came from a painful break up. Memories can help us heal but, they can also become obstacles to our moving forward. Consciously select which mementos you choose to keep. Some mementos will uplift and help to maintain positive, healthy memories others may bring up painful times and delay our ability to move on.

2. This is a good time to bring new energy into your home. Consider rearranging the furniture. Bring in some fresh flowers or new plants. We often have a difficult time sleeping during stressful endings. So, get new bedding, hang some new pictures in the bedroom, make some uplifting changes. Make your entire living space a peaceful and inviting place to relax, heal, grow, and prosper.

3. Be conscious of self-care during times of change and transition. It is easy to neglect ourselves during this time.
   - Be sure to eat.
   - Eat healthily.
   - Get some exercise even if it's just a walk a few times a week.
   - Maintain your physical bodily cleanliness, in fact take extra care physically, go beyond your usual.
   - Wear clothing with bright colors.

- Stay in contact with friends, family and your spiritual community; avoid any tendency to isolate yourself from others.
- If you feel yourself falling into depression, get professional help. We get help to stay healthy and strong, not because we are weak.
- This is not the time to make major life decisions without professional advice and the friendly advice of at least one very close friend or family member. When we are grieving some kind of loss or major life change our judgment may not be at its best.
- Find a hobby or some fun activity to get involved in. The more you keep your mind busy with pleasant activities, the less time you have to linger in the painful past.

4. Music can help with release as well. Find songs that have lyrics uplifting to you. In fact, this is a good time to monitor the music you do listen to. Songs that tell of others who are in pain won't help you heal and will most likely extend your time of grief. Remember you want to be free from any holding on to what is finished, and that which is causing you to feel hurt, lonely, abandoned, afraid, or unworthy.

*Releasing methods for the inner work of letting go and moving on from a relationship that is in transition.*

1. Write a letter to the individual regarding what you need to release. You may need to release anger, fear, thoughts of lack, etc. Write the letter to the person letting them know that you have decided to release yourself from the bondage of painful memories and any negative emotions associated with them. After the letter is written place it in an envelope, read Psalm 23, 3 times and place the letter in your Bible for 3 days. On the third day, tear it up into very small pieces, place it in its own trash bag and then throw the bag into your main trash bag.

After a week, if painful thoughts continue to come up at the same rate, repeat this process again in order to make the release stick in your mind. You'll know when the release is occurring for you, you'll be able to think about the person without the heavy feeling of emotional pain.

2. Make a list to burn. On a sheet of paper, list all that you desire to release. Do not list people. Only mention names in regard to the painful thoughts, feelings, emotional attachments and any resentments you hold toward them. Use your own words to address your situation, but here are a few examples to get you started:

- *"I now release all feelings of anger I have toward _____ regarding our divorce."*
- *"I now release all thoughts of revenge and anger I have toward _____ for firing me from _____ company."*
- *"I now unbind _____ (person's name) from any negativity I have been holding toward him/her. I willingly, easily, and lovingly release him/her to the good that awaits him/her and now we are both free to embrace our highest good."*
- *"I now set myself free from any bondage to the situation regarding _____. From this point forward, I go freely and easily to enjoy the good that awaits me."*
- *"I now let go of all feelings of regret, guilt, jealousy and fear toward _____. I am ready to move forward, free to enjoy the good God has in store for me."*

When your list is done, read it over once, affirm that you have the strength to release, and mentally let go all that you have listed, and then burn it. Watch the paper turn to ashes and know that you have made a conscious decision to let go. As the fire dies down, affirm that the release in you is complete.

3. Write affirmative statements in your journal. These are positive statements about how you see yourself after you have fully embraced the change and moved on to enjoy your life. Do this daily for 21 or 40 days. Write your own, but here are a few examples to get you started. Notice we are not affirming anything particularly related to

338

the release. That's because you want to see yourself having moved beyond it.

- *"I am a child of God. I am healthy, happy, and blessed in every way. I enjoy the life I am living."*
- *"I feel blessed that I am fully living a happy, fulfilling life."*
- *"I love myself and I love the life I am living."*
- *"I feel vibrantly alive and enjoy the people in my life, as they enjoy being with me."*

4. Meditate on the verse from Psalm 51:10. It is a verse that can be recited, prayed and written to help do inner emotional and mental cleansing. Find an affirmative statement that addresses your prayer desires, or write one of your own, and say it often. Here are two variations of the same affirmative statement. I have used it successfully and have recommended it to others many times:

- *"I love myself enough to let go of what is finished and complete. In this way I am a magnet for healthy, happy, and prosperous new beginnings."*
- *"I love myself enough to let go of what is finished and complete. In this way I am a magnet for wonderful new opportunities and glorious new possibilities."*

Finally, set about preparing yourself for new beginnings. If indeed a new beginning is on your horizon, get ready in every way that you can for its successful arrival in your life. If you've experienced a job loss, then start getting ready for the new job that is on the way. If your best friend has moved away, start a plan to meet new friends or set goals to visit the friend that has moved away.

Remember to always pray for a smooth letting go process and a joyous moving forward experience. Label all your new beginnings as blessed and expect it to be so.

339

As our capacity for God-centered friendship unfolds, we enjoy expressing it with others - this is true friendship.

# 47

## *Thank God for Friends*

*Prayer Anchor:* *"Now when Job's three friends heard of all these troubles that had come upon him, each of them set out from his home...They met together to go and console and comfort him. When they saw him from a distance, they did not recognize him, and they raised their voices and wept aloud; they tore their robes and threw dust in the air upon their heads. They sat with him on the ground seven days and seven nights, and no one spoke a word to him, for they saw that his suffering was very great" (Job 2:11-13).*

The Book of Job opens up by telling us that Job was the man who had it all. Job had a good relationship with God, lived his life as a God-centered man, had great prosperity and success in the land where he lived, and a family that he loved a great deal. By the time we reach Chapter 2 of the Book, Job, the man who seemed to have it all, was hit with great devastation and what we might call personal tragedy. Much of his wealth was gone in an instant, all his children had been killed, and then Job himself was struck with a bodily disfiguring illness - all this, on the same day.

Certainly in the Book of Job, we find many lessons from which we may learn. However, the part of the story that quickly draws my attention is the caliber of friendships that Job has formed. Job's 3 friends come to his side quickly. When they first get a glimpse of Job from a distance, he is so disfigured that they don't seem to recognize him. Not concerned if his illness was contagious or afraid to look at his disfigurement, they proceed to be near him.

They express their grief for Job. They wept aloud, tore their robes and threw dust on their heads. This was their showing of sympathy, sadness and sorrow with and for their friend. And then they did

343

something that demonstrates a high caliber of friendship. They sat with Job in total silence for 7 days and 7 nights. Their first show of support was their presence. They showed up for Job just to be at his side; in silence they all sat with Job for 7 days and 7 nights.

There is quite a difference in knowing someone and being a friend to someone. Job's 3 friends are beyond just knowing him. Their commitment and loyalty suggest that they share a deep care, concern and love for each other. They sit with Job just the way he is, for what he is, just as they found him on that very difficult day. A friend loves us just the way we are, believing that we will grow through our challenges. "A friend loves at all times" (Proverbs 17:17).

Our lives are rich, full, and blessed when we cultivate friendships where love, respect, integrity and honesty are the foundation. There is no greater gift to compare with the gift God has given humankind than each other.

We are fashioned after God and designed to love and care for each other. Through prayer and meditation we develop the pure expression of friendship with God. "Thus the Lord used to speak to Moses face to face, as one speaks to a friend" (Exodus 33:11). **As our capacity for God-centered friendship unfolds, we enjoy expressing it with others - this is true friendship.** As we develop our own friendship with God through living a God-centered life, we become the living expressions of God's love we were created to be.

God has given us the gift of each other, with the idea of friendship that we may enjoy, nurture and grow together in unity and love. We take every opportunity to cultivate meaningful relationships not for what they can do for us; we know we don't have to concern ourselves with the return of our friendship. The law of giving and receiving handles this for us. The love we give out will surely be returned to us, multiplied. We engage ourselves in harmonious, healthy, God-centered friendships for the gift of sharing God's love with others. Thank God for friends!

## *Prayer Practice*

Cultivate friendships by being a good friend. "Some friends play at friendship, but a true friend sticks closer than one's nearest kin" (Proverbs 18:24). Pray with and for your friends. Spend time with them expressing the best of who you are. Allow your friends to get to know you, and make yourself available to know them. Always hold your friends in high regard. Think, speak, and see Truth for and about them. When you pray for them, affirm only the truth about who and what they are. As you live and model this kind of God-centered friendship, the same caliber of friendship will be returned to you.

You may never need your friends to sit in silence with you for 7 days and nights as Job did. However, most of us at some time in our lives will need and appreciate the care and concern of people we call our friends. A true friend is one you can ask to pray with you and that you should be willing to pray with also.

So, from time to time, ask your friends if there is something that you could pray with them about. Let them know if you have a prayer desire that they can hold for you. You may feel that because you are close it goes without saying that you keep each other in prayer, but say it anyway. It is a great reminder of the caliber of friendship you have when you occasionally ask, "May I pray with you about anything in particular? You're always on my prayer list, but I thought I would ask." "I do not call you servants any longer, because the servant does not know what the master is doing; but I have called you friends, because I have made known to you everything that I have heard from my Father" (John 15:15).

When you gather with your friends, have a brief prayer together. It doesn't have to be long and flowing. Even a brief time of connecting together in God can have powerful affect on our friendships and on the prayer that we pray together. Join with friends to experience some of the prayer practices in this book and then celebrate your friendships by sharing the powerful results.

*Prayer is powerful when we are still, as well as when we are moving.*

# 48
## Pray and Move your Feet

### Prayer Anchor: *"For we walk by faith, not by sight" (2 Corinthians 5:7).*

When our church first bought our current site, it was an avocado grove with about 374 trees on it. We were so grateful for the demonstration of our own land upon which to build our church that we wanted to bless the land and everything upon it. We began taking prayer walks each Saturday morning for about 6 months (The Miami heat would not allow us to do the prayer walks in the summer months). There would be anywhere from 5 to 15 people who would show up dressed in sweats ready to walk and pray. We would have a specific prayer to pray ranging from a scripture to some affirmative prayer that had been pre-selected. We would have a group prayer before beginning the journey and then, we would set out walking and praying in single file around the 5 acres of the property.

We walked for about an hour each time. After the walk, we would gather on the patio, drink lots of water, and then share what we experienced on our walk. It was always a gift to hear how answers had been revealed, fresh new ideas discovered, and gratitude filled the hearts of those who had made a one-hour journey around the property focusing on God, focusing on good.

We were not too surprised when the avocado crop came in that first year more abundant than the property had ever produced. The company that maintained the grove for the previous 10 years said to us at harvest time, "I don't know what you people did, but this is the most abundant avocado crop we've ever seen on this property." Our prayers had blessed us, and the land upon which we walked and prayed had been abundantly blessed as well. It was indeed a double spiritual gift.

A walk outdoors can be uplifting in and of itself. The body needs exercise and fresh air; walking outdoors helps to clear the mind.

349

When you walk outdoors, you have the opportunity to enjoy God's handiwork in nature. Being outdoors can have a way of helping us to remember that God's power is greater than what we can imagine or do of our human selves. Remember when God asked Job the question, "Where were you when I laid the foundation of the earth? ...Have you commanded the morning since your days began, and caused the dawn to know its place, so that it might take hold of the skirts of the earth?..." (Job 38:4, 12, 13).

There is just something about the beauty of nature that humbles us. And when we are humble, we are teachable, Spirit will guide us and our humility prepares us to listen inwardly. "Teach me your way, O Lord, that I may walk in your truth; give me an undivided heart to revere your name" (Psalm 86:11).

To pray and walk, or to take a prayer walk, can be a metaphor for what it means to "walk by faith and not by sight." When we walk by faith, we move forward, we do not let our thoughts linger in the outer appearances of what we see with our physical sight. We move forward with our plans, our dreams, and our goals in the expectancy of drawing on the good which already exists in the invisible realm.

When we move our feet we are in action toward our desires, not looking at outer circumstances but trusting that with each step we take it is right, perfect, and in divine order. When we take a prayer walk, we immerse ourselves in the consciousness of praying and moving forward as the powerful movement of Spirit within us and on behalf of that for which we pray.

A moving prayer, an active prayer, also spreads many blessings for that which comes into the range of consciousness of the prayer. Just as the trees felt the healing, loving energy of the prayers that we prayed as we walked around the church property, so did the two dogs we encountered week after week. Our neighbor to the north of the property had two large dogs. When we first started walking the perimeter of the property we would come close to the fence where these two dogs were quietly at rest until we came near. For the first few months whenever we would get close to the fence, they would both begin jumping and barking in a fierce manner. After we had passed by they would relax and rest again. Well after several months these two dogs were as quiet as little lambs as we walked by. They would stand up, look, watch each one of us go by without barking and then lay back down. It was as if they could feel the loving prayer energy we were radiating.

**Prayer is powerful when we are still, as well as when we are moving.** This particular prayer process invites you to set a conscious time of prayer while actively moving your feet in a walk stride. Most of us are very familiar with praying and being still, but to walk and consciously pray; is a bit different. "...the Lord appeared to Abram and said to him, 'I am God Almighty; walk before me, and be blameless'" (Genesis 17:1). As you move taking steps on the outer, know that Spirit is moving in your behalf within you toward the realization of your desires.

## *Prayer Practice*

Walk and Pray. The idea is to set your prayerful thoughts toward your desire and move your feet! Do this outdoors if possible so that you get the added blessing of engaging nature on your journey. You set your own intention, make it a faith walk, a love walk, a peace walk, a joy walk, a prosperity walk; you name the kind of thoughts you will hold in your consciousness as you walk.

Take your walk with the realization that God is within you as you make your prayerful journey. Set your intention to "walk blameless before God." This says that your thoughts will be without error and focused on truth, faith, life, love and wisdom. Decide that you will have an open mind to the divine ideas that are sure to be revealed to you on your journey. Expect possibilities to be made known to you during this time. Walk with the truth that "With God all things are possible", the expectation that your faith in God brings answers, and divine blessings will surely come.

You may use a particular affirmation or scripture that focuses on your faith in God. You may print it on a "4 x 6" card to carry it with you or commit it to memory. You decide on what prayer best suits you or simply let your prayers flow from your heart. You may even decide to let Spirit put a prayer in your heart as you begin your walk. The important thing is to be open and focus your attention on God, life, truth, and divine ideas, then walk.

Where to walk? Find a park, a site near a lake, a place that has a walking trail where you will not be disturbed by heavy traffic to distract your attention away from your walk with God. You may find a place that has a walking path that has been intricately designed with sacred geometry such as a labyrinth. Any place with beautiful scenery will be especially nourishing to your spirit as you walk and pray. Go forth, pray, and move your feet.

*Make a commitment today to never again conform to the outer limitations lurking in the day-to-day activities we mistakenly call our lives.*

# 49
## Pray up the Life You Desire

**_Prayer Anchor:_** _"Do not be conformed to this world, but be transformed by the renewing of your minds, so that you may discern what is the will of God-what is good and acceptable and perfect" (Romans 12:2)._

The theme that runs through this book is that everything we think, say, and do represents prayer. The beauty of this principle is that we get to create the life we desire. By our prayers, we get to participate in the unfolding of the life we want, the person we want to be, and the things we want to do.

Daily we face our former thoughts, words and deeds that have made their way into manifestation. We planted them into our hearts and minds as seeds in earlier times. We allowed them to grow and grow and grow by giving them space to take root in our minds. We nourished them with the inner beliefs we held toward them. And now we face them – good, not so good or indifferent. The good news is that we may now consciously use this same process to create what we choose to face in the tomorrows of our days.

Our prayer anchor for this chapter gives a compelling message on how we are to use our thoughts, words and prayer power to create the life we desire. It lets us know we should never just accept the way things appear as the way they must always be. We are not to be conformed to the small plans that others have adopted for themselves.

Life is huge, expansive, grand, and it should be experienced in a major way. The language of the scripture is strong: "Do not be conformed to this world." Sometimes it takes a firm stance to understand just how important words of truth are to our health, prosperity, and well-being. We are given this message in a forceful way because it will require from most of us a great deal of practice, training, and study to actually follow these powerful instructions that indeed have the capacity to change our lives for the better.

We are accustomed to believing what we see with our eyes. We like to check the facts and figures of what has already been done. We like knowing past history before we make a decision to move forward. We love to engage the opinions of others. And certainly there is a time and place for these actions. But our scripture tells us not to "conform" to all the data gathering we do in conjunction with the purpose of moving our lives forward. We are to follow a path that will lead us to "the will of God - what is good and acceptable and perfect." And anyone reading a book on prayer certainly is seeking this path.

Our challenge, however, is that we must overcome our early childhood conditioning. We were taught from childhood to conform. The child who has a difficult time in the educational system is the one who has his/her own ideas. Generally Children are not taught to have their own ideas, or to think creatively. Life is easier for the child who learns to conform early in life. Children do not generally like being singled out for being "different" from their peers. This early childhood conformity robs young people of the creative possibilities that the mind was designed to express. Our mind capacity to dream, vision, create, and take on the seeming impossible goes largely unused unless we heed the words of our prayer anchor. Through prayer, we position ourselves to move beyond the conformed ways the world thinks and renew our minds in the life, love, and wisdom of God.

Conformity can be fatalistic thinking. This often shows up like doing what has always been done without being open to other possibilities. We should ask ourselves "does this way of thinking honor our God-given gifts of imagination, faith, power, wisdom, strength, and zeal? Many of us are content with a few trinkets that imitate happiness, rather than claim the true happiness we all so richly deserve. God has given us a mind with which we may make choices and decisions based on our individual expression of wisdom and creativity. When we get out of the conforming mind set we are ready to take on transformation.